T0293801

The Corporate Social Responsibility Agenda

The Case for Sustainable and Responsible Business

The Corporate Social Responsibility Agenda

The Case for Sustainable and Responsible Business

Olivier Delbard

ESCP Europe Business School, France

World Scientific

NEW JERSEY · LONDON · SINGAPORE · BEIJING · SHANGHAI · HONG KONG · TAIPEI · CHENNAI · TOKYO

Published by

World Scientific Publishing Co. Pte. Ltd.
5 Toh Tuck Link, Singapore 596224
USA office: 27 Warren Street, Suite 401-402, Hackensack, NJ 07601
UK office: 57 Shelton Street, Covent Garden, London WC2H 9HE

Library of Congress Cataloging-in-Publication Data
Names: Delbard, Olivier, author.
Title: The corporate social responsibility agenda : the case for sustainable and
    responsible business / Olivier Delbard.
Description: New Jersey : World Scientific Publishing Company, [2020] |
    Includes bibliographical references.
Identifiers: LCCN 2019049781 (print) | ISBN 9789811206597 (hardback)
Subjects: LCSH: Social responsibility of business.
Classification: LCC HD60 .D37 2020 (print) | DDC 658.4/08--dc23
LC record available at https://lccn.loc.gov/2019049781

British Library Cataloguing-in-Publication Data
A catalogue record for this book is available from the British Library.

Art cover: Copyright Adeline Ruel/Atelier des Noyers

For any available supplementary material, please visit
https://www.worldscientific.com/worldscibooks/10.1142/11451#t=suppl

Desk Editor: Daniele Lee

Typeset by Stallion Press
Email: enquiries@stallionpress.com

ACKNOWLEDGMENTS

First I would like to thank David Sharp, Senior Editor at World Scientific for his constant support.

I would also like to thank Jamie Wiens for her useful comments and suggestions.

To my students, for their feedback and inspiration.

Finally, my love and gratitude go to Claire, Marie and Quentin.

"We are each part of the web of life — the continuum of humanity, sure, but to a larger sense, the web of life itself. We have a choice to make during our brief visit to this beautiful blue and green living planet. We can hurt it or we can help it. For you, it is your choice".

Ray Anderson,
Founder and former CEO of Carpet Tile Manufacturer Interface,
Inc., 2011

"We have a decade to act before the economic cost of current viable solutions becomes too high. Without action, we risk catastrophic and perhaps irreversible changes to our life-support system. Our primary goal must be to take planetary responsibility for this risk, rather than placing in jeopardy the welfare of future generations".

Elinor Ostrom, Nobel Prize in Economics, June 12, 2012

"Without a sense of purpose, no company, either public or private, can achieve its full potential. It will ultimately lose the license to operate from key stakeholders. It will succumb to short-term pressures to distribute earnings, and, in the process, sacrifice investments in employee development, innovation, and capital expenditures that are necessary for long-term growth. It will remain exposed to activist campaigns that articulate a clearer goal, even if that goal serves only the shortest and narrowest of objectives".

Larry Fink, CEO of Blackrock,
world's largest asset management company,
Letter to CEOs, January 2018

CONTENTS

LIST OF FIGURES

INTRODUCTION

The context

We live in an open world in which information circulates constantly and where mass travel has never been so easy. A globalized world which affords material wellbeing to an ever-growing number of people whose life expectancy keeps increasing.

But we also live in a world in which social inequalities are growing, both at a global and local level. According to a recent report, inequalities have grown exponentially in the last decade. One telling example is the fact that the number of billionaires has doubled since the 2008 financial crisis and the top 26 billionaires are now worth 1.4 trillion dollars, which is equal to the income of 3.8 billion people,[1] i.e. half of the world's population! Around 830 million people still live in extreme poverty, i.e. on less than $1.25 a day, and 80% of the world population on less than $10 a day. This is also a world in which famine, civil wars and terrorism are forcing millions of people into exile.

Our planet itself is under threat: the latest reports[2] alarmingly show that climate change caused by human activity is reaching highly dangerous levels, threatening our lives and economic models. Our activity is causing irreversible damage to ecosystems, the rate of loss of biodiversity is so rapid that some scientists are calling it the *"sixth wave of*

---

[1] *Public Good or Private Wealth?*, Oxfam International Report, Jan. 2019.
[2] See the 2018 *IPCC Report–Summary for Policy Makers*, https://report.ipcc.ch/sr15/pdf/sr15_spm_final.pdf

extinction".[3] Nature's ecosystems services, such as insect pollination, are in real jeopardy. In addition, we have overexploited renewable and non-renewable resources: July 29th 2019 was the Earth Overshoot Day One meaning *"the date when we (all of humanity) have used more from nature than our planet can renew in the entire year"*.[4]

One might say that governments and international institutions are responsible for these threats to our environment, for governments are the ones in charge of ensuring the common good and can thus pass legislation and sign international treaties aiming at making our planet livable and sustainable. One may also wonder about the role of the business community in responding to these pressing social and environmental issues.

According to a well-known phrase, *"the business of business is business"*, indeed, the role of businesses is to provide products and services, thus contributing to the economy through the jobs they create and the taxes they pay. Businesses generate profit which in turn contributes to furthering investment and development. As for their owners, naturally they expect the best financial returns possible; this is especially the case of joint-stock companies whose owners are the shareholders who have entrusted professionals with the management of their companies.

This book refutes this idea: Today the business of business is obviously NOT ONLY business. Faced with mounting social and environmental risks, the business world has its share of responsibility in finding solutions to make the planet more livable and sustainable.

Furthermore, when one looks at the top 100 richest entities in the world today, less than one-third are States... while more than two-thirds are multinational corporations! A recent survey conducted by a team of University of Amsterdam researchers[5] concluded that out of the top 100 economic entities based on revenues, there were only 29 States while the leading corporation Walmart ranked 10th!

These social and environmental responsibilities that businesses need to take are usually what defines corporate social responsibility (CSR).

---

[3] See Elizabeth Kolbert, *The Sixth Extinction–An Unnatural History*, Picador, 2014.
[4] From www.overshootday.org
[5] Babic, Heemskerk & Fichner, "Who is more powerful? States or corporations?", *The Conversation*, July 2018.

Even though the CSR concept has existed for 60 years, it is only really in the last decade that it has spread across the world and become a mainstream management-related concept, and as some would say a new buzzword. CSR is now taught in business schools around the world and never have there been so many research papers written on the subject. Yet, given the multitude of related practices and perspectives, CSR lacks a clear definition.

This might account for why there is so much skepticism about CSR today: what difference is there between CSR which is merely P.R. greenwashing and CSR issues that are embedded into the core strategy of a company? In other words, what differentiates between cosmetic and strategic approaches?

In this book, though keeping this dichotomy in mind, we will not focus on greenwashing and socialwashing abuses. Instead we will emphasize concrete cases that demonstrate the willingness of businesses to move toward a strategic approach to CSR. This choice is grounded in the firm belief that embedding CSR issues into corporate strategy is the only way for businesses to be resilient and remain legitimate, maintaining their "license to operate" in the medium- and long-term while offering tangible and efficient responses to the mounting sustainability challenges that are affecting our planet.

Many significant changes have taken place over the last decade, confirming the increasing pressure placed on business to adopt sustainability-related policies. The pressure comes both from society at large and various institutions. A global civil society is taking shape: citizens around the world are more actively involved in working toward a better future and they expect businesses to contribute to finding solutions to social and environmental ills. More and more consumers are ready to boycott products which may cause harm to their health and to the environment. Even though consumer awareness is particularly present in the developed world, activism is now increasingly spreading to the developing world, due to sanitary and ecological scandals directly affecting local populations.

This global civil society is stronger than ever thanks to sophisticated information and communication technologies, NGOs, watchdog associations and grassroots movements that challenge businesses and put pressure on them to change their behaviors and practices. In addition, information about social, environmental and ethical practices is readily available almost everywhere. With regard to the media, they also play a considerable role and are always keen to expose bad corporate behaviors and practices…

Thus, companies are increasingly realizing that their reputation may be at stake if they do not take measures to improve their social and environmental performance. Now when faced with a crisis, businesses tend to respond more rapidly and more resolutely. One example is the Danish company Lego which decided in 2014 to stop selling its Lego brick boxes in all U.K.-based Shell service station shops after a Greenpeace campaign denounced the oil and gas giant's decision to drill for oil in the Arctic. This resulted in huge revenue losses for Lego.[6] Another example is that of the cement multinational LafargeHolcim whose CEO was forced to resign in 2017 after it was proven that the company had not ceased its operations in Syria and had also conducted illegal deals with terrorist organization ISIS.

Yet, our aim is not to target any particular company: we must bear in mind that the risk of unethical conduct is omnipresent and that all businesses will likely be confronted with social, environmental or ethical scandals at some point. Even the most virtuous and sustainability-driven companies may find themselves accused of animal cruelty, pollution hazards, labor-related issues or unethical business conduct![7]

On the institutional side, a major turning point was the launch of the 17 Sustainable Development Goals by the U.N. in 2015.

These goals agreed upon by the international community each have certain precise quantified targets to achieve by 2030. The innovative aspect of this U.N.-sponsored scheme is that involves every key player on the planet, from national governments to NGOs to the private sector. Aligned with the ten principles of the U.N. Global Compact, these economic, social and environmental goals provide businesses with a formidable opportunity to adopt sustainability-related practices.

Goal 17 on partnerships is especially important for businesses since it aims at strengthening cooperation between public and private actors regarding common issues. As a result, several multi-stakeholder coalitions

---

[6] Estimated at around 65 million pounds per year.
[7] Patagonia, The Body Shop, Adidas and LafargeHolcim respectively.

Figure 1: The 17 U.N. Sustainable development goals

have emerged, such as the Food and Land Use coalition which includes U.N. agencies, NGOs, expert groups and multinational companies such as Unilever and Yara.

Although it is too early to measure the true impact of these goals, one can only hope that they will really serve as tangible instruments which will facilitate companies around the world in moving forward in their CSR endeavors.

The objectives

This book's key objective is to assess the state of CSR today while focusing on some of the more critical related issues. This requires first examining the roots and scope of CSR and then where and how it has developed over time and how it has resulted in a new form of CSR that encompasses a broad and diverse range of social, environmental and ethical issues companies now face.

Analyzing and questioning the actions and policies of businesses in the field of social responsibility will lead us to examine and explore CSR-related concepts such as philanthropy and sustainability.

But before delving into the different forms of CSR, a simple and generic definition can be provided simply by examining the three letters of CSR:

— C stands for Corporate, meaning that the concept of CSR is strictly reserved for corporate forms of business. For other organizations such as governments, NGOs, social enterprises, etc., the term "social responsibility" is preferable.
— S stands for Social, and this encompasses a broad range of issues related to people (including both employees and the community at large) and to the planet, (meaning the natural environment) to ethical issues such as corruption, lobbying and the need for transparency.
— R stands for Responsibility, which in this case takes on a much broader meaning. Firstly, a distinction must be made between responsibility and liability, and this clearly indicates that CSR is voluntary rather than just a legal requirement.

Even more importantly, CSR today is *extended over time and space*: in *time*, since ecological issues such as climate change are forcing companies to take responsibility now for tomorrow, in other words companies are taking responsible actions today for what might otherwise occur in the future.[8] The responsibility is also extended over *space* since a company may now be considered socially responsible outside of its legal boundaries; for example, a multinational corporation having outsourced all of its production is deemed socially responsible for the actions of its subcontractors and suppliers.

This book is divided into six main chapters.

The first chapter provides an understanding of the genesis and historical development of CSR, from Bowen's seminal book in 1953 to the most recent theoretical developments. The first part gives an overview of the main theories and schools of CSR whereas the second part proposes a practical approach to CSR embeddedness, from philanthropy to strategic CSR.

---

[8] This new ethics of responsibility was theoreticized by German philosopher Hans Jonas.

The second chapter deals with the stakeholder issue. Stakeholders are inextricably linked to CSR since the latter is based on the assumption that companies need to take into account the social expectations of the various stakeholders with whom they engage. After showing how the stakeholder theory developed and was first implemented, this chapter aims to show that stakeholder inclusion remains a practical challenge for companies. In other words, "walking the talk" on stakeholder inclusion is an uphill climb...

Chapter Three focuses on a central dimension of CSR which often remains overlooked: though it is generally accepted that employees are central to CSR matters, the reality is somewhat different, especially when it comes to acknowledging the importance of employee representatives as CSR stakeholders. For us, this question is clearly a "blind spot" which needs to be given more attention.

Chapter Four deals with the question of human rights, a fairly recent item on the CSR agenda which is rapidly taking a very prominent place in the CSR debate. It can even be said that human rights may soon be one of the most crucial issues for businesses in the world today.

Chapter Five deals with critical environmental issues and how businesses can learn sustainability from nature and drastically improve their environmental performance, thereby moving away from CSR-as-usual to sustainable strategies. In the last section of this chapter, we will focus on one specific case, that of the U.S. carpet manufacturer Interface, which is one of the best, if not the best example of a company that is fully committed to sustainability today.

The sixth and last chapter broadens the perspective on CSR by examining some key issues for its future. Based on a few key assumptions, we will draw the contours of tomorrow's CSR with a special focus on corporate sustainability as the promising "post-CSR" approach. In the second part of this chapter, we will stress how important it is for consumer citizens to put pressure on businesses to go further and scale new heights to devise genuine, efficient social responsibility strategies.

Finally, it must be noted that this book is the reflection of my own experience with CSR over the years. Even though I am quite familiar with CSR within the U.S. context, I have opted for a European perspective in this book, all the more so as I was educated in Europe and have worked there most of my adult life. My interest in the developing world is evidenced by the insertion of many examples of and reflections about CSR in developing countries, even though it remains difficult to assess what form their CSR will take.

I have scrupulously chosen cases and examples from diverse cultural backgrounds and industries. This I felt was absolutely essential. This book does not claim, however, to provide a fully comprehensive overview of CSR today. For a number of reasons, certain dimensions were given priority while others have been somewhat left aside. I hope the reader will understand the inherent logic of this choice after reading the book.

CHAPTER 1

TOWARDS CSR EMBEDDEDNESS — FROM THEORY TO PRACTICE

I always start a new CSR course by asking students the following questions: What does CSR mean to you? What form does it take? The most common answers by far are: "Charities, donations to communities", especially among non-European students. This, I believe, reflects the most widespread view on CSR today: Corporate social responsibility is little more than a well-packaged, updated version of good old philanthropy which has existed for ages in many places around the world. So is CSR ultimately just a rebranded version of a long-established business practice? This could partly explain the skepticism surrounding CSR, all too often viewed as a mere corporate public relations exercise aimed at embellishing the facade...

Here lies a major paradox if we take the definition of CSR provided by the European Union in 2011[1]:

> *"To fully meet their corporate social responsibility, enterprises should have in place a process to integrate social, environmental, ethical and human rights concerns into their business operations and core strategy in close collaboration with their stakeholders."*

This definition of CSR clearly has nothing to do with corporate philanthropy. On the contrary, it calls for the *embeddedness* of CSR issues,

---

[1] European Commission, 2011.

be they social, environmental, ethical, human rights or consumer-related into corporate strategy and operations. Why then is there such a discrepancy between the commonly held views on CSR and the current institutional expectations pertaining to it?

CSR seems to be a hazy and controversial concept in its very essence. At least 37 definitions of CSR have been identified lately![2] This introductory chapter provides a tentative answer to the following question: Has CSR moved beyond corporate philanthropy for certain, or is it the same old philanthropy in the guise of a new marketing gimmick? In other words, is the CSR of today and tomorrow likely to be radically diffferent from what it has been in the past, or will it remain, in one way or another, a charity-based contribution to society? The central question will then be that of the "embeddedness" of CSR, i.e. its *permanent integration* into corporate strategies and operations, and more largely speaking, into society at large.

To answer this question, this chapter is divided into two complementary sections. First, we will examine how the CSR concept was gradually "institutionalized", why it originated in the U.S., and how the concept has evolved over time and space, leading to the emergence of a European-style type of CSR which is quite distinct from the "original" U.S.-born CSR. We shall examine the institutionalization of CSR, meaning here its embeddedness in society, through a review of the main theoretical approaches which have been proposed since its inception in the 1950s in the U.S. Our main preoccupation will be to study whether or not CSR is departing from traditional forms of corporate ethics and philanthropy, thus leading to an ambitious new integrative approach.

The second section will move from theory to practice by looking at the actual implementation process of CSR and the various steps leading to its embeddedness. Our objective will be to demonstrate why moving beyond philanthropy is crucial for modern corporations so that CSR becomes an efficient tool to meet society's demands and expectations, in other words: a fully legimitate concept in the eyes of all parties.

---

[2]Dahlsrud A.: "How Corporate Social Responsibility is Defined: an Analysis of 37 Definitions", *Corporate Social Responsibility and Environmental Management*, 2006.

1. The institutionalization of the CSR concept

1.1. *Howard Bowen's book social responsibilities of the businessman: Seminal and visionary*

"The day of plunder, human exploitation, and financial chicanery by private businessmen has largely passed. And the day when profit maximisation was the sole criterion of business success is rapidly fading. We are entering an era when private business will be judged solely in terms of its demonstrable contribution to the general welfare".[3]

The year 1953 is usually referred to as the date of birth of the concept of "corporate social responsibility". Indeed, a book entitled *The Social Responsibilities of the Businessman* was published that year in the U.S. Its author, Howard Bowen, a welfare economist, had been commissioned by the National Council of Churches (an association of Protestant denominations) to write a book on "ethics and the economic life", sponsored by the Rockefeller Foundation.

Although this book is constantly referred to in academic literature on CSR, it appears that very few people have actually read it in full,[4] which is a pity, given its relevance and modernity regarding the current debates over CSR.

Although the debate over whether corporations should maximize profit for the sake of their stockholders or make business decisions combining economic and social objectives had been going on since the 1920s,[5] Bowen wrote his book at a time when major changes were taking place among U.S. business leaders about the role of business in society. After decades during which a laissez-faire ideology marked by the domination of stockholders' interests over social issues[6] had been the clear winner, an

---

[3] Bowen, p. 52.
[4] The book remained out of print for a long time.
[5] For instance, in 1957, Heald emphasized the emergence of a "corporate conscience" among large U.S. corporations in the 1920s and the development of "humane and constructive policies as well". (p. 37).
[6] See the 1919 Michigan Court decision "Dodge vs Ford Motor Company", which ruled that Henry Ford had to manage the company in the stockholders' interest, rather than in a charitable manner benefitting his employees or customers.

impressive number of large U.S. corporation CEOs were now publicy advocating for the need for business leaders to find the right balance between the interests of the owners and those of other "interested parties". For instance, Frank Abrams, the CEO of Standard Oil of New Jersey, declared in a public address in 1951 that:

> *"The job of management is to maintain an equitable and working balance among the claims of the various directly affected interest groups... stockholders, employees, customers, and the public at large. Business managers are gaining professional status partly because they see in their work the basic responsibilities [to the public] that other professional men have long recognized as theirs".*

Even though one may question the concrete implications of such public positions, they do reflect the prevailing state of mind in the more democratic post-war U.S. society where corporations were expected to take their share of responsibility and contribute actively to society's welfare; in other words they were to act *responsibly* toward society. With the rising influence of some categories of "interest groups" such as consumers or labor unions, a few corporations had started to issue their own codes of conduct in which they publicly stated their responsibilities toward different interest groups; a famous example being provided by Johnson & Johnson's *Credo*, written as early as 1943.[7] While many were, and still are, skeptical about the concrete implications of such documents, Bowen had in his book already gone one step further, stating his wish for these codes to become "more specific and concrete".[8]

The changes in the American society at the time may be explained not only by the sociological evolutions of post World War II America but also by the rapid growth of corporations and their changing governance structures. With the ever-increasing need for capital, the time when the owner was the manager was over: "Professional businessmen", as they were called, were now in charge of running the corporations on behalf of the owners, while being held more and more accountable for the impacts of

---

[7] See Chapter 2.
[8] Bowen, p. 161.

their decisions on society at large. This gradually led to the debate over the agency dilemma, i.e. the separation between owners and managers, and the ensuing principal-agent relationship. However, in the 1950s there was a large consensus on the fact that managers ought to be serving the interests of both stockholders and society as a whole. It must also be said that these new professionals were coming from more diverse backgrounds, with closer ties to other aspects of society. They simply could not ignore the growing expectations of a modern democratic society.

While on the whole being representative of these changes, Bowen's book clearly demonstrates the fundamental role of cultural and religious tradition in the shaping of corporate social responsibility. One full chapter is dedicated to the influence of Protestantism and its fundamental beliefs in the principles of *trusteeship* and *stewardship*, as demonstrated in the following excerpt:

> *"Those who own property have the duty of using and administering it, not exclusively for their own purposes, but in ways that will serve the needs of the whole society. From the moral point of view, there must be no such thing as unrestricted and irresponsible ownership. The owner is a trustee accountable to God and society".*[9]

According to this concept, anyone will be rewarded by God if he/she acts in the interest of his/her brethren, meaning that acting on behalf of the common good and sharing the fruits of success are fundamental to a righteous life. Following these religious precepts, *trusteeship* and *stewardship* became two key principles of the U.S. Protestant work ethic upon which is based Bowen's view of the social responsibility of businessmen: Serving as trustees, businessmen are to be accountable for their deeds to society. Acting as stewards, their role is to serve and administer in the best interests of society. Well ahead of his time, Bowen even extended the notion of stewardship to the preservation of natural resources.

The influence of religion on the emergence of CSR in the U.S. is crucial because it establishes a clear link between the responsibilities of businessmen and their personal ethics. In this respect, Bowen perpetuates

---

[9] Bowen, p. 33.

the long-standing tradition of business ethics in the U.S., embodied by the overarching principle of doing good for one's community. This is, for example, what steel magnate Andrew Carnegie proclaimed in his famous *Gospel of Wealth* in the late XIXth century:

> *"This, then, is held to be the duty of the man of Wealth: First, to set an example of modest, unostentatious living, shunning display or extravagance; to provide moderately for the legitimate wants of those dependent upon him; and, after doing so, to consider all surplus revenues which come to him simply as trust funds, which he is called upon to administer, and strictly bound as a matter of duty to administer in the manner which, in his judgment, is best calculated to produce the most beneficial results for the community — the man of wealth thus becoming the mere agent and trustee for his poorer brethren, bringing to their service his superior wisdom, experience and ability to administer, doing for them better than they would or could do for themselves".*[10]

Carnegie's ethical stance is representative of the corporate philanthropy which was developing in the U.S. at the time.[11] Deep-rooted in religious belief, philanthropy calls for a moral engagement of the businessperson toward his/her community. To put it simply, "he/she who succeeds shall share part of his success with society". From then on, corporate philanthropy took the form of corporate donations given by businesses and managed by them, either directly or, more often, through foundations. In other words, "giving back" became the golden rule.

When one reads his book carefully, it appears that Bowen, while acknowledging the relevance of philanthropic activities, goes even further by advocating a new type of philanthropy which would transcend "purely altruistic" motives and serve business interests *per se*:

> *"But community activities are thought of not only in purely altruistic terms. Businessmen feel that a good reputation in the community is good business. It enhances employee morale and general public relations.*

---

[10] Andrew Carnegie, *Wealth*, 1889.
[11] Whereas corporate philanthropy was limited by law for many decades in the U.S., it finally became common practice at the end of the XIXth century.

It helps to create a favorable labor supply in the community and to enlist the cooperation of community leaders and officials".[12]

This is where Bowen's book remains fully relevant today: While clearly connecting corporate social responsibility to traditional business ethics and philanthropy and their religious origin, Bowen widens the scope of social responsibility, expressing visionary views on the role of business in society. From then on, the definition of CSR has transcended traditional philanthropy.

As a matter of fact, Bowen realized the role CSR can play in enhancing the reputation and performance of corporations in the U.S. As the passage quoted above shows, a socially responsible business generates several benefits, be it in terms of public image ("general public relations"), human resources ("labor supply") or good relations with public authorities. If the question of the need for competent labor was a topical issue at the time, Bowen was also aware of the positive correlation between widening the scope of social responsibility and strengthening corporate performance through its reputational capital. He even anticipated the future need for a specific function in the company: *"Some day ... a new official known as the 'manager of the department of social responsibility'"*.[13] It would take at least four decades before the advent of CSR managers, the beginnings of which were evidenced most notably in Europe.[14]

Bowen tackled an impressive number of other still topical issues in his book, such as the need for the proper training of professional managers in business schools, and the necessity of carrying out social audits in corporations. He was fully aware of the need to institutionalize the role of various "stakeholders" (the word was still unknown at the time) by having independent Board members, creating "industry councils". In modern terms, his approach to CSR has a lot in common with today's

---

[12] Bowen, p. 63.

[13] Bowen, p. 155: *"Some day, a new official known as the 'manager of the department of social responsibility' might be created to coordinate the activities of the various officials who represent various aspects of the public interest".*

[14] France was one of the first countries to generalize the practice due to a 2001 law that compelled publicly listed companies to report on their social and environmental performance.

neo-institutionalism. As Jean-Philippe Gond stated in the introduction to the new edition, a fundamental question in Bowen's book is: "*What is the proper mix of voluntary initiative and coercive pressure most likely to align corporate activities with public interest*"?[15]

Finally, and even more strikingly, Bowen insisted on the need to think long-term, which according to him is the only way of reconciling stock-holders' and society's interests. Basing his rationale on sound business logic, he was convinced that the new generation of professionals would undoubtedly take the long-term into account in order to sustain their business performance.

And this leads to the most astonishing fact about the book: Bowen had understood the need for environmental and social sustainability more than thirty years before the actual concept of sustainable development was even coined. Here is what he stated:

> "*Another range of questions centers around the responsibilities of a business toward future generations as distinct from the present generation. How rapidly and in what manner should it utilize nonreplaceable natural resources? What provision should be made for the replacement of timber, fish and other reproducible natural resources? Is the destruction of arable land through strip mining ethically defensible... It can be argued that it is desirable for a business to take a long view in its decisions, because a long view is likely to coincide more nearly with social interests than is a short view. It can also be argued that obviously wasteful use of natural resources is morally indefensible, and that businessmen should be continuously searching for more economical methods of using them and striving to find reproducible substitutes. In general, however, there are limits to the expenditures, or forbearance, which can reasonably be expected of businessmen. Consequently, the interests of future generations probably must be handled largely through governmental policy — with which businessmen should be expected to cooperate*".[16]

In short, Bowen's book provides contemporary readers with a fundamental understanding of CSR, both for yesterday and today. On the one

---

[15] Gond, p. xiv.
[16] Bowen, p. 227.

hand, *Social Responsibilities of the Businessman* appears as the first comprehensive and normative attempt in the field of CSR, prolonging the already well-established practices of corporate philanthropy and business ethics. On the other hand, the book displays a truly visionary conception of the role of CSR towards society, anticipating future debates over sustainability, long-term performance and the political role of corporations.

1.2. The theoretical development of CSR in the U.S. (1950s–1990s): Multiple and contradictory

As pointed out by present-day academics,[17] the CSR literature in the decades following Bowen's book seems rather poor and disappointing. Even though some new schools of thought did appear, as we will see below, the theoretical debates were mainly focused on philosophical and ethical issues: How can businesses find the right compromise between economic performance and ethical conduct? From purely liberal views on business responsibility, CSR appeared as a utilitarian device at best. Bowen's visionary views seemed to have fallen into oblivion...

1.2.1. The 1950s and 60s: Profit only?

Indeed, Bowen's vision did not prevail in the Fififties and Sixties in the U.S. A fierce ideological debate over the purpose of business had already forced Bowen to resign from his university position because his social responsibility views were judged too "anti-business", this happening during the dark years of MacCarthyism. The liberal view held by Levitt and Friedman was definitely taking the lead, signalling a striking return to the "profit only" view of business. As Levitt proclaimed in 1958:

> *"Welfare and society are not the corporation's business. Its business is making money, not sweet music".*[18]

The "sweet music" Levitt was referring to became pure evil in the eyes of future Nobel Prize economist Milton Friedman. According to

---

[17] See for instance Carroll, 1979, Acquier & Aggeri, 2008.

[18] Levitt T.: "The Dangers of social responsibility", *Harvard Business Review*, 1958.

Friedman, any attempt by managers to spend money on social responsibility went against the interest of the stockholders, who, as owners, were clearly hoping to maximize their return. Hence, the sole responsibility of managers was to make profit, as a famous article published in the *New York Times* in 1970 claimed. For Friedman, a distinct wall had to be erected between the corporate world and society: If managers wanted to support social responsibility initiatives, they could very well do so by voting for "socially-oriented" politicians or by donating money to private charities.

While Friedman's neo-classical agenda is grounded on a pure and perfect value maximisation model, it does include the basic "rules of the game". His theory perfectly illustrates the most liberal view on CSR: As long as businesses comply with the law and carry out their activities "without deception or fraud", they are "socially responsible"! Yet, Friedman's view should not be so easily discarded; he did rightly point out the inherent flaws of philanthropy at the time he was developing his theory. His view became the mainstream approach to business for a long time, right up until renewed CSR approaches and a fast-changing world started to make it sound "obsolete". But more on that later.

1.2.2. 1970s–1990s: A changing society, renewed CSR approaches

The following decades were characterized by very contradictory trends in the U.S. society: While the liberal school of CSR remained quite strong in business circles, some alternative CSR theories were being developed. To some extent, the emergence of new approaches to CSR reflects the radical evolution of American society in the 1970s: The anti-nuclear, environmental, pacifist, feminist and hippie movements, among others, were clearly indicative of a major shift in society toward social and environmental concerns. The future of the planet as well as respect for minorities were emerging as key demands from society.

These new aspirations among the youth had already appeared in the Sixties; two highly mediatized events perfectly illustrate the emergence of an active civil society ready to put pressure on business and industry. The first case refers to the book by U.S. biologist Rachel Carson published in

1962 entitled *Silent Spring*, in which she denounces the harmful effects of pesticides, notably DDT, on people's health and the environment. The chemical industry reacted harshly against Carson, accusing her of falsifying scientific evidence. After a few months' debate, the accuracy of Carson's findings was proven, leading to a complete ban in 1972 by the U.S. Administration of DDT in agriculture. The whole affair had a tremendous impact both on public opinion and public policy. It was most likely responsible for the creation of a federal agency in charge of the environment, namely the Environmental Protection Agency (EPA) which was established in 1972.

The second case is linked to the publication in 1965 of another book, *Unsafe at Any Speed*, by Ralph Nader. A lawyer, Nader was criticizing the big U.S. carmakers of voluntarily ignoring safety issues in the making of their cars (with a focus on Chevrolet's *Corvair*). Fiercely attacked and intimidated by the industry, Nader finally won his case when the Federal Administration started legislating on safety requirements as of 1966. As for the industry, the carmakers themselves eventually recognized the need to put more emphasis on safety.

These two events were decisive: Not only did they trigger legislative responses from the Federal Government in the U.S., but they also prompted businesses to start taking social and environmental concerns into account in their operations.

From a regulatory perspective, the 1970s became known as the "environmental decade" in the U.S.: The first Earth Day was celebrated in 1970, Greenpeace was created the following year, 1972 marked the birth of the EPA, the first U.N. Conference on the Human Environment was held in Stockholm, and major federal regulations were passed in the following years (new *Clean Air Act* in 1970, *Endangered Species Act* in 1973, *Safe Drinking Water Act* in 1974, *Clean Water Act* in 1977 to name a few). On the social front, the fight against discrimination and the inclusion of minorities were becoming major concerns on the political agenda.

These profound social changes obviously led to a much more critical view of corporations by society, which also prompted a new generation of management thinkers to tackle the CSR question in an innovative and constructive manner. CSR started to be revisited, with new pragmatic attempts made to reconcile economic and social objectives. In the face of predominantly liberal business practices, these CSR approaches were clearly *instrumental* and/or *utilitarian*,[19] as analyzed later by academics endeavoring to "map" the conceptual CSR territory. These approaches were also much more *managerial*[20] in essence, departing from the traditional philosophical/ethical/liberal view.

At the same time, some large U.S. corporations were starting to include these new social and environmental issues in their managerial agendas. This is clearly apparent in the first new significant CSR approaches embodied by the *Corporate Social Responsiveness* theories as developed by Ackerman and Bauer[21] in the 1970s. By corporate social *responsiveness*, these academics meant first how organizations become aware of and respond to social issues in a pragmatic way, as opposed to the corporate social *responsibility* concept deemed too abstract. Responsiveness is based on a dual approach: On the one hand, it deals with how companies respond individually to social issues; on the other hand, it aims at investigating the factors that determine the social issues to which businesses should respond.

The corporate social responsiveness approach opened the way to pragmatic managerial CSR theories focused on the real-life daily interactions between businesses and society. The new focus was on managers' ability to be responsive to social issues and find ways of addressing these issues with the appropriate corporate responses. In a very innovative way, Ackerman and Bauer called for an "agenda for a humanized society" and for the need to learn to "institutionalize novelty". Ackerman also developed a model whereby companies would be able to find the appropriate solution by adopting a life-cycle analysis of a social issue, from problem recognition and study to the actual implementation of solutions.

Even though the proposed model looks largely obsolete today due to its mechanicist and reductionist nature, the corporate social responsiveness movement did play a decisive role in establishing a clear link between

---

[19] Garriga & Melé, 2004; Capron, 2011.
[20] See for instance Acquier & Aggeri, 2008.
[21] Ackerman & Bauer, 1976.

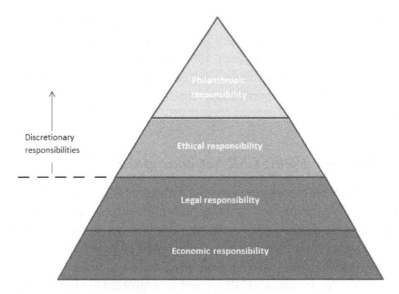

Figure 2:   From Carroll's pyramid

the managerial operational and social issues agendas. It also paved the way for the future *Corporate Social Performance* approaches focused on social impacts, programs and policies.[22]

Another step was taken in the 1970s with the emergence of the *integrative* CSR approach represented among others by Carroll.[23] In his famous pyramid, Carroll proposed to integrate the two commonly accepted responsibilities of business, namely the economic and legal responsibilities, and the ethical and philanthropic responsibilities, in addition to the first two and representing the CSR agenda based on ethics and philanthropy.

Carroll's theoretical construct clearly aimed at merging the liberal and instrumental views on CSR, reflecting a growing trend among U.S. corporations to think in terms of their multiple responsibilities, ranging from core to voluntary. Carroll's input enabled to theorize the establishment of a comprehensive approach to responsibility, eventually leading to a value maximization conception of CSR.

---

[22] See for instance Wood, 1991.
[23] Carroll, 1979.

This pragmatic approach to CSR was backed up by another decisive theory also reflecting the changes in the society, the *stakeholder theory* embodied by Freeman in the early 1980s. We will come back in detail to this theory in the following chapter, but needless to say that the emergence of the stakeholder concept definitely contributed to shaping today's CSR approaches.

1.3. Since the 1990s: CSR has gone global

In the 1990s, CSR literature was prolific, but seemed to be constantly revolving around the same issues, bringing little more than added confusion. It looked as if the concept would forever be torn between the liberal view and diverse instrumental and utilitarian approaches proposed by academics. Despite some innovative theoretical advances and the growing focus on corporate social "performance", CSR seemed to be doomed to remain a utilitarian tool used by companies on a discretionary basis and relying mostly on "home-made" business ethics and traditional philanthropy.

Most strikingly, CSR still remained an almost purely Anglo-Saxon concern, mostly developed in the U.S., with some forays into the U.K. Only in the late 1990s-early 2000s did new schools of thought appear, with teams of researchers working on CSR in the U.K. and in continental Europe, bringing along a fresh outsider's perspective to the concept. They were naturally bound to adopt a comparative approach to CSR in order to understand why the concept was essentially North American and how it could be adapted to other parts of the world.

One of the best demonstrations of this new trend was provided by Matten and Moon's seminal paper published in 2008, in which they argued that CSR was "explicit" in the U.S., whereas it had remained largely "implicit" in the rest of the world. Adopting an institutionalist approach, Matten and Moon meant by "explicit" that:

> *"U.S.-style CSR has been embedded in a system that leaves more incentive and opportunity for corporations to take comparatively explicit responsibility".*[24]

---

[24] Matten & Moon, p. 409.

They went on to define explicit CSR as:

"Corporate policies that assume and articulate responsibility for some societal interests. They normally consist of voluntary programs and strategies by corporations that combine social and business value and address issues perceived as being part of the social responsibility of the company".[25]

This accurately reflects what we have observed so far regarding the institutionalization process of CSR in the U.S. CSR was obviously born and raised as a "for the U.S. only" concept and is inextricably linked to the political institutional development of the country from the late 19th century to the 1950s when the term officially appeared. Let us not forget that Bowen himself had clearly expressed the fact that his study was relevant only for large corporations operating in the U.S.

Conversely, *implicit* CSR was defined by Matten & Moon as the:

"Values, norms and rules that result in (mandatory and customary) requirements for corporations to address stakeholder issues and that define proper obligations of corporate actors in collective rather than individual terms".[26]

CSR in Europe had thus remained largely implicit, which does not mean that corporations were not expected to behave in a socially responsible way, but that these expectations were implicit, due to the highly different institutional settings. The term CSR itself appeared rather late in continental Europe, with some research showing that CSR in 2011 in Germany was still considered a non-relevant concept by most stakeholders.[27] Through the explicit vs implicit debate, Matten and Moon were justifying both the "innate" relation between CSR and the U.S., and also anticipating the emergence of a European-style CSR generated by other actors such as the business world.

---

[25] *Ibid.*
[26] *Ibid.*
[27] Delbard 2011.

1.3.1. *The rise of institutional theories*

The need for a social contextualization of CSR was felt strongly by European researchers because of the obviously different settings and stakeholder expectations among national cultural and institutional models across Europe and the world. The *National Business Systems* theories largely contributed to this conceptualization: NBS theories were developed in the 1990s with a view to offering a relevant and comprehensive model to analyze institutional systems. By identifying five key subsystems, political, financial, educational, labor-related, and cultural, NBS theories provided a fine-grained view of different institutional settings.[28]

The European approach to CSR experienced a very rapid development in the 2000s: Several schools of thought appeared, including the Francophone (mostly in France[29] and Quebec[30]), Germanic and British schools. Whereas the Francophone school largely emphasized its divergence with U.S.-style CSR theories and the Germanic school focused on neo-institutional approaches, the English school, while paving the way for an institutional understanding of CSR, attempted to bridge the theoretical gap with U.S.-based approaches. All in all, European research definitely brought fresh new insights which would in turn inspire future research on CSR all around the world.

Paradoxically enough, the emergence of a European school of CSR highlighting its specificity resulting from different institutional frameworks was rapidly compounded with a neo-institutional approach essentially based on the analysis of the fast-changing global environment. Indeed, European research on CSR developed in the late 1990s-early 2000s, at a time when the world was experiencing a major turning point in its history, with the end of the Cold War and the acceleration of the globalization process.

As early as 1983, Di Maggio and Powell evidenced the trend toward homogenization among organizations, leading to the theory of institutional isomorphism, defined according to three complementary dimensions:

---

[28] For NBS theories, see Whitley 1992, 1997, 1999, 2002.
[29] Led by pioneers Capron, Igalens and a few others.
[30] The "School of Montreal" represented by Gendron, Pasquero among others.

Isomorphism is first *normative*, due to the growing standardization of practices, skills and networks among organizations. It is then *mimetic*: In a context of bounded rationality, organizations tend to imitate each other and adopt the same policies. Finally, isomorphism is *coercive*, especially due to the evergrowing influence and pressure exerted by the State and other public actors onto organizations.

This theoretical breakthrough was proof that a dual and contradictory evolution of CSR was taking place, with the homogenization of corporate practices due to globalization on the one hand, and the need to stress local differences due to specific institutional settings on the other.

This is also what Matten and Moon expressed when contending that CSR in Europe was becoming more and more "explicit", due to government impulse (talking about the "enabling" State), the homogenization of institutional environments and the "Americanization" of management practices in a globalized world.

The input of institutional approaches proved decisive in spreading the concept of CSR around the world. It contributed to alternative approaches to CSR which are able to better reflect non-Anglo-Saxon corporate realities, while acknowledging for the most part the globalization process at play and the pivotal influence of Anglo-Saxon practices.

1.3.2. A turning point: Sustainable development and the triple-bottom line approach

A major disruption in the development of CSR was brought about by the concept of sustainable development which was officially introduced in 1987 with the well-known Brundtland Report commissioned by the U.N. Backed up by a rising ecological awareness instigated by the scientific community and the civil society, sustainable development was first a diplomatic concept aimed at finding a new development path which would be suited to the newly emerging open and globalized world.[31]

Sponsored by the U.N., sustainable development was initially designed for political actors, from the international level down to the

---

[31] Delbard, 2014.

regional, national and local levels. The Rio Conference held in 1992 largely confirmed this, with most of the Heads of State of the planet gathered to commit to a more sustainable world. In fact, up until the end of the XXth century, sustainable development was mostly viewed as a cultural, political and scientific concept... With no direct implications for business! Apart from a few well-identified "green champions", mostly from the Anglo-Saxon world (The Body Shop and Ben & Jerry's for instance), the business world staunchly believed that sustainable development was an issue for public decision-makers and regulators, and definitely not for businesses engaged in a tougher and tougher globalization battle.

The link between sustainable development and business started to began to appear at the turn of the century. From an international perspective, the World Summit on the Environment held in Johannesburg in 2002 marked the official appearance of business players. Indeed, many large corporation CEOs attended the conference, along with many international NGO representatives. So-called "Type II" agreements were signed between corporations and NGOs, marking the beginning of partnerships of a new type focused on the sustainability agenda. Concomitantly, the European Union launched its Göteborg strategy in 2001, putting sustainability at the heart of its overall strategy for 2020.

The same year, with a view to "promoting a European framework for corporate social responsibility", the European Commission issued its first official definition of CSR:

> *"A concept whereby companies integrate social and environmental concerns in their business operations and in their interactions with their stakeholders on a voluntary basis".*[32]

The European Union was the first major political entity to officially endorse CSR, adopting a strong sustainability-driven orientation. Indeed, "integrating social and environmental concerns into business operations" is nothing else but the transposition of the sustainable development objectives into the business sphere. As a matter of fact, this officially marked the distinctiveness of European-style CSR, grounded on sustainability.

---

[32] *European Commission Green Paper*, 2001.

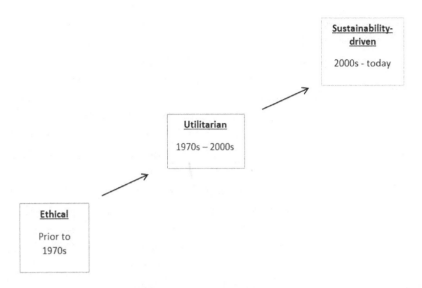

Figure 3: The key drivers of CSR

This European specificity is no doubt related to the research on CSR and sustainability which flourished on the Old Continent in the 1990s. Furthermore, the institutional approach probably facilitated the linkage between CSR and the political decision-making sphere. From then on, CSR would clearly take on a distinct flavor in Europe.

As explained by French academic Michel Capron,[33] Western Europe actually initiated the third wave of explicit CSR: After the first *ethical* wave in the U.S. occurring during the XXth century up until the 1950s, the second *utilitarian* wave in the U.S. from the 1970s to the 1990s, *sustainability-driven* CSR marked a new wave, mostly to be found in Europe, characterized by the embeddedness of CSR into business and society at large.

Indeed, Bowen had already stressed the need for socially responsible corporations to adopt a long-term view, especially regarding the use of natural resources. But Europe no doubt embedded sustainability into CSR in a more systematic way: analyzing business school CSR education (teaching and research) across Europe, Matten & Moon demonstrated in their 2004 paper that apart from its business ethics dimension, CSR

---

[33] Capron, 2011.

education in Europe was significantly grounded on the environmental agenda, including both an earlier approach based on "environmental concerns" and the post-1990s "sustainability". Interestingly enough, the expression CSR itself was not used so much by European business schools. This may be explained by the relative novelty of the concept at the time in Europe and also by the "institutional embeddedness" of CSR at play.

One of the major breakthroughs leading to sustainability-driven CSR was provided by Elkington's "triple bottom line" concept in 1997. John Elkington, founder of SustainAbility, one of the first sustainability consulting firms established in 1994, proposed the triple bottom line approach as the operational application of sustainability to the business world. Elkington called for a three-dimensional approach, declaring that sustainable development is built upon three main dimensions: Economic, social and environmental. Later on, the catchy "People, Planet, Profits" slogan came to embody the triple bottom line approach and it is still widely used by corporations today.[34]

The triple bottom line approach rests on the assumption that corporate performance should not be measured in economic and financial terms only, but on the contrary, should include what are traditionally thought to be "externalities", namely social and environmental issues. In other words, sustainability relies on a company's ability to report on its social and environmnental performance, along with the traditional economic performance, ultimately leading to one unified three-dimensional performance encompassing all the dimensions. This obviously necessitates the creation of new indicators; as a matter of fact, Elkington has always been a strong proponent of the full cost approach in accounting.

Elkington clearly adopted a business-focused perspective, choosing performance as the cornerstone of social responsibility. His approach is linked to the intangible capital concept, i.e. the necessity for businesses to include their natural, technological, social and human capital in their valuation methods. As a result, the triple bottom line approach is also focused on both business ethics (at the junction between the economic and social dimensions) and environmental justice (at the junction between the environmental and social dimensions).

---

[34] Shell was one of the first companies to officially endorse the slogan in the early 2000s.

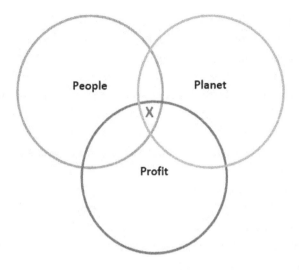

Figure 4:   The triple bottom line (from Elkington, 1997)

While the triple bottom line appears to be a very attractive concept (particularly for practitioners), it is worth stressing the fact that very little academic research has been conducted on the concept itself. Whereas many point out its difficult implementation and lack of effectiveness, it is clear that it has been largely endorsed not only by companies around the world, but also by NGOs and international institutions or initiatives (e.g. the GRI, WBCSD, etc.).[35] Yet, it is criticized both by the radical left thinkers and environmentalists, who reject the very notion of natural capital and its reductionist economic view, and economic liberals who caution against the dangers inherent in wishing to align environmental, social and economic dimensions in business.

In any case, the triple bottom line has been instrumental in connecting business with sustainability, in the wake of the corporate social performance approaches from the 1990s in the U.S., and bridging the gap to some extent between U.S.-style and European-style CSR, the former emphasizing the ethical implications of CSR while the latter pushes forward the implicit political agenda.

---

[35] See below.

The blended value proposition defended by Jed Emerson[36] is worth mentioning at this point, since Emerson's assumption is based on the fact that value creation is intrinsically made up of more than one dimension. Emerson worked mostly on non-profits, showing that corporations also needed to take economic factors into account when measuring their performance. If we look at it the other way around, for-profit corporations ought to take non-economic indicators into account. Emerson's theory in that respect is therefore quite similar to Elkington's triple bottom line.

Elkington's triple bottom line exemplifies what started to be depicted as the "market for virtue".[37] By coining this phrase in 2006, Vogel wanted to reveal a somewhat darker side of CSR and sustainability that should not be overlooked: For Vogel, despite some tangible progress having been achieved thanks to CSR (notably in the field of labor or environmental impact), the adoption of CSR by companies in the U.S. and Europe has not been all that efficient, and has instead led to the creation of a new market, a niche market, where "virtue", in this case "social responsibility", has become an opportunity to do business and generate revenues while having no, or very little, broader impact, on society.

By this, Vogel was referring to all the new standards, norms, and related services, such as accreditation, certification, consulting, etc. available. Though this less convincing development of CSR deserved to be mentioned, we feel nevertheless that too pessimistic a view on CSR could be detrimental in the longer run, since it is *de facto* discarding all the positive aspects brought about by the deployment of CSR over the last few decades. In any case, the limits of current CSR approaches remain, and Vogel rightly reminds us of the absolute necessity to remain critical about CSR and how it is actually implemented!

1.3.3. Since 2000: From corporate citizenship to political CSR?

The sustainability-driven wave of CSR undoubtedly prompted new theoretical debates: with CSR clearly drifting away from an ethical-utilitarian

---

[36] See Emerson, 2005.
[37] See Vogel, 2006.

perspective and moving into more core business-related issues, the question of the new role of corporations in a globalized society is becoming more and more acute.

A new step was taken with the notion of "corporate citizenship": whereas the idea that the corporation ought to behave as a good citizen had been firmly grounded in U.S.-style CSR from the start, a new school of thought in the early 2000s came up with a renewed conception of citizenship. In a context of globalization of management practices, business networks and value chains, Logsdon & Wood in 2002 were among the first to theorize corporate citizenship as the cornerstone of CSR in a globalized world. Introducing the concept of "global business citizenship", they stressed the need for corporations to behave as citizens wherever they operate, thus paying attention to the need to adapt to local cultural environments.

While departing from the traditionally vague conception of corporate citizenship, Logsdon & Wood's view remains very much in line with the U.S.-style philanthropic approach to CSR. Besides, they explicitly stated this when they defined the "new corporate citizen" as:

"a responsible player in its local environments ... [with an] [e]mphasis on voluntarism and charity, as well as on the organization's rights and duties in and for the community".[38]

Although positively received, this approach was largely criticized by the European school of CSR. Emphasizing the need for a normative approach to citizenship, Moon, Matten & Crane in 2005 offered a fresh invigorating analysis, providing a broader and more ambitious definition of corporate citizenship. To put it simply, their approach contended that the role of corporations had to evolve from "being a good citizen" to "protecting citizenship" by contributing to rule-making and the provision of public (common) goods.

The question was no longer for corporations to behave *like* citizens but to *be* citizens. With this assumption, the European institutionalist school was taking a radical step, acknowledging the role of corporations

---

[38] Logsdon & Wood, (2002), p. 156.

in the political-legal-institutional field, and thereby breaking away from the sacrosanct "isolationist" view of business.[39]

What Matten, Moon & Crane are advocating is a renewed institutional approach in the wake of globalization. This so-called *neo*-institutional approach was further developed by Scherer & Palazzo (2008), representing the "Germanic school" of CSR, rooted in the German school of philosophy (Jürgen Habermas) and sociology (Ulrich Beck).

Scherer & Palazzo provide a thorough analysis of the consequences of globalization, as well as the institutionalizing process of CSR. According to them, the globalization process that is gaining momentum is having a drastic impact on institutional settings, and consequently on social demands.

Following Beck's analyses, they first pointed out the emerging "meta-power" of corporations that have become "quasi-states". Secondly, they stressed the fact that national States around the world are by and large unable to address global social and environmental issues. And thirdly, they insisted on the evergrowing influence of NGOs and civil society on a global scale.[40] These trends are evidenced by the rising involvement of corporations in international institutions and fora, in which they are gradually becoming full-fledged actors alongside governments and civil sociey organizations.[41]

Compounded with the wave of financial scandals such as Enron in the early 2000s, this analysis based on three converging trends leads Scherer & Palazzo to posit that this evolution entails changing social expectations worldwide and that:

> *"Companies are expected to become socially committed even in areas not directly related to their business or the efficient supply of goods".*[42]

---

[39] By "isolationist", we mean the view according to which the "purpose of business is business", i.e. that business should in no case interfere with political institutional issues.

[40] Scherer & Palazzo, 2008.

[41] See for instance the WBCSD (*World Business Council for Sustainable Development*), the GRI (*Global Reporting Initiative*) and the various U.N.-sponsored initiatives and summits.

[42] Scherer & Palazzo, 2007, p. 1097.

The neo-institutionalists are thus calling for a "politically enlarged conceptualization of CSR". Scherer & Palazzo's objective is to offer a countermodel to the dominant liberal model which urges corporations to behave ethically and respond to the demands of local communities. They justify corporations behaving as political actors as well as economic actors through a convincing analysis of the globalization process which is currently reshuffling the respective roles of institutional actors and the business world:

> "*The globalizing society erodes established ideas about the division of labor between political and economic actors and calls for a fresh view on the role of business in society. These phenomena need to be embedded in a new concept of the business firm as an economic and a political actor in market societies*".[43]

In a context of weakened political actors and new global societal demands, they call for a "politicization" of the corporation. This shift is correlated to the rise of a global civil society through NGOs, and more generally to the need for renewed legitimacy for corporations. It is time for corporations to embrace a more proactive attitude in solving issues pertaining to the common good:

> "*For a corporation to deal with changing societal demands in a reasonable way, it must replace implicit compliance with assumed societal norms and expectations with an explicit participation in public processes of political will formation. We consider this shift the politicization of the corporation*".[44]

Yet, neo-institutionalists cannot ignore the strong pressures exerted by the market and individual interests in our societies. That is why they base their model on the Habermasian "deliberative democracy". In the 1990s, German philosopher Jürgen Habermas started to develop an applied

---

[43] *Ibid.*, p. 1115.
[44] Scherer, A. & Palazzo, G.: "Toward a Political Conception of Corporate Responsibility: Business and Society Seen from a Habermasian Perspective", *The Academy of Management Review*, Vol. 32, N°. 4, 2007, p. 1098.

model of decision-making that enabled corporations to move beyond self-interest and reach solutions for common good problems through deliberative approaches.[45] Scherer & Palazzo believe that corporations as well as other institutional players have to "play this new game".

One concrete implication of the deliberative democracy approach is the necessity for corporations to be transparent and accountable to society, by providing tangible objectives and concrete results on societal issues, the inherent risks being green- and socialwashing. Obviously, some large international corporations are becoming more and more engaged in concrete social and environmental policies, from access to water to promoting female empowerment. Yet, these policies are frequently contradicted by unethical decisions or, more generally, overall corporate policies. Many CSR reports lack coherence and materiality, thus often keeping the reader "lost in translation"!

The underlying assumption here is that corporations will find it genuinely in their own interest to take on a proactive "political" role in society. As critics and skeptics rightly deplore the all too often deceptive engagement of corporations, strategically incarnated visions remain key to "walking the talk".

This radically new conception of CSR known today as "political CSR" is having far-reaching consequences on the new role corporations can play in addressing CSR-related issues around the world. While being strongly challenged by the still dominant liberal view, political CSR is gaining ground, especially in Western Europe and some parts of the developing world. Besides, the 17 new sustainable development goals established in 2015 by the U.N.'s "Agenda 2030" appear to be a real opportunity to consolidate the political role of corporations.

1.3.4. The liberal response in the 2000s

Faced with the "politicized" European approach to CSR, the U.S.-born liberal approach started to be re-examined in the 2000s, with a view to reconciling value maximization and societal demands. The key drivers to

---

[45] See for instance *Between Facts and Norms: Contributions to a Discourse Theory of Law and Democracy*, 1992.

these new liberal approaches were mainly the globalization process, the loss of legitimacy for corporations and the need to adapt traditional philanthropy to a culturally open and diverse world.

1.3.4.1. Porter & Kramer and the shared value concept

Corporate strategy guru Michael Porter and his colleague Mark Kramer were the first to advocate a radical evolution. Building upon the competitive advantage theory, Porter & Kramer departed from Friedman's view by positing that to be efficient, CSR had to be embedded in the company's strategy. In their 2002 paper focused on philanthropy, Porter & Kramer called for a new strategic philanthropy, as opposed to the current practice described as *"diffuse and unfocused"*. They went further by discarding the current evolution of philanthropic activities seen as close to little more than mere greenwashing campaigns:

> *"Increasingly, philanthropy is used as a form of public relations or advertising, promoting a company's image or brand through case-related marketing or other high-profile sponsorships".*[46]

While still adhering to the U.S.-style philanthropy-based CSR, Porter & Kramer promoted a strategically aligned form of philanthropy which would provide corporations with new competite advantage opportunities in diverse environments, thus creating value.

They went much further in their 2006 and 2011 papers: First, in 2006, they developed a new typology, including the Porterian value chain concept. This led them to distinguish between "responsive CSR" based on the traditional "good citizenship" along with value chain mitigation efforts on the one hand, and "strategic CSR" taking two forms: value chain transformation and "strategic philanthropy". While still focusing on the philanthropic dimension of CSR, Porter & Kramer played a decisive role in aligning CSR with the entire value chain. This had a major impact on mainstreaming CSR, by embedding it into corporate strategic objectives.

---

[46] Porter M. & Kramer M.: "The Competitive Advantage of Corporate Philanthropy", *Harvard Business Review*, Winter 2002.

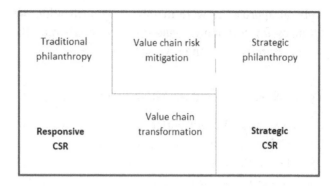

Figure 5:   Responsive vs strategic CSR (from Porter & Kramer, 2006)

Porter & Kramer also focused on what motivates corporations to engage in CSR by distinguishing between four main approaches: 1) The *moral imperative*, i.e. CSR motivated by ethical considerations, such as the traditional U.S.-style approach; 2) The *license to operate*, when corporations seek legitimacy from society before engaging in socially and/or environmentally hazardous activities, such as in extractive industries; 3) *Reputation*, when CSR becomes an element of the brand and/or intangible capital, such as in consumer-goods industries; 4) *Sustainability*, when long-term environmental sustainability is at the core of the CSR approach, such as in "big impact" activities. This typology is indeed useful since it helps understand the level of commitment of corporations and the type of CSR they are likely to engage in. It can be noted that ethical as well as instrumental and sustainability-driven forms of CSR are recognized by Porter & Kramer.

In 2011, Porter & Kramer took a major step forward, moving beyond the CSR concept to launch Corporate Shared Value (CSV). The shared value concept is a smart approach to value maximization since it aims at bridging the gap between value creation and societal issues by assuming that creating value for society (by responding to unmet social demands in developed or developing countries) will in turn create financial value. For the first time in the liberal sphere of thought, profit-making and CSR were not at odds; on the contrary they could be mutually self-reinforcing!

Porter & Kramer's great strength was to provide an operational framework for implementing shared value. They articulated it around three main priorities: 1) *Reconceiving products and markets* by identifying social problems for which responding to consumers and contributing to the common good might be achieved in parallel; 2) *Redefining productivity in the value chain* by simultaneously addressing the social, environmental, and economic issues related to supply chain actors; and 3) *Enabling local cluster development* in order to meet several development objectives in cooperation with local institutional and business actors.

In what became an extension of the 2006 paper, the shared valued concept had a tremendous impact on the business as well as academic communities. It must be acknowledged that Porter & Kramer offer a very attractive framework, speaking the practitioner's language while putting forward concrete solutions for building up the "conscious capitalism" of the XXIst century. In a nutshell, shared value seems to be offering a concrete win–win solution, the best of both worlds...

Appealing though it may be, Porter & Kramer's approach does raise some more critical questions, some of which were mentioned in a paper written in 2014 by some prominent neo-institutionalists.[47] While recognizing the positive contribution of Porter and Kramer, they developed a series of critical points which appear to be quite relevant: first, they rejected the innovative dimension of shared value by showing that many researchers had already shown the necessary interconnection between financial value and social issues. Second, they insisted on the fact that Porter and Kramer had neglected the complexity of the world in which corporations operate by ignoring the inherent tensions between economic and social issues in day-to-day corporate strategies and decision-making processes. Finally, they blamed the shared value concept for being far too "corporate-centric", i.e. solely based on individual corporate interests. To illustrate this point, it seems that Porter & Kramer were more interested in the shared value programs *per se*, even when initiated by multinationals whose products or services are not socially responsible, rather than in the long-term potential of some multi-stakeholder initiatives whose common good objectives surpass individual private value maximization efforts! One must recognize that most of the examples cited come from

---

[47] Crane *et al.*, "Contesting the value of creating 'shared value'", 2014.

corporations that are not necessarily considered the most virtuous in terms of products or corporate culture...[48]

More generally speaking, Porter and Kramer offer a rather shallow conception of the corporation's role in society. According to Crane *et al.*:

> *"While CSV might be a good way of integrating various activities into one social strategy, it fails to deliver orientation for a responsible corporate-wide strategy. It thus fails in Porter and Kramer's aim to redefine the purpose of the corporation".*[49]

This debate does not come as a surprise: two antagonistic views on "embedded CSR" are clearly expressed. On one side, Porter and Kramer are seeking to resolve the conflict between profitability and CSR by proposing to solve some critical social and environmental issues and boost profitability. In other words, they manage to "rebrand" liberal capitalism, without altering the rules, and to redesign CSR without deviating from a deep-rooted U.S. perspective.

On the other side, the neo-institutional European approach pushes the corporation beyond its traditional sphere: relying on a transdisciplinary approach (not only management science but also social and political science, philosophy, anthropology, etc.), it assigns a political role to the corporation in addition to its economic role. CSR thus becomes the foundation for a new type of corporate legitimacy, providing solutions for the common good on the planet *on top of* the corporate value creation generated by the original raison d'être of business which is to put a product or a service on the market.

Two brands of CSR are emerging: one, embodied by Michael Porter, is better suited to practitioners, as it speaks their language. The other one, originating in Western Europe, may not be as practical or as easily implementable but raises fundamental questions about the future of corporations in an open complex world in which traditional institutional players are losing importance and influence. We will attempt to modestly put forward a "third way" by proposing a "convergent" approach in the next section of this book.

---

[48] Like Swiss multinational Nestlé or Yara, a Norwegian fertilizer company.
[49] Crane *et al.*, p. 137.

1.3.4.2. The Bottom of Pyramid approach

Among other new liberal approaches, the Bottom of Pyramid (BOP) theory developed by C.K. Prahalad[50] is worth discussing at this point. The BOP approach stems from a striking fact: when looking at the world pyramid of wealth, we see that just 1% of the population owns 50% of the overall wealth, while about 2.7 billion people live on less than 2.5 dollars a day, among whom 1.25 billion live on less than 1.25 dollar a day, which is the extreme poverty line.[51]

While being clearly liberal in its essence, Prahalad's theory rests on a fairly innovative assumption: for him the bottom of the pyramid population, i.e. those more than 2.7 billion people in the world, are consumers whose demands are not properly met and who often find themselves the victims of unsafe low-quality and overpriced goods and services. He rightly points out that charity-based approaches to the poor often prove to be inefficient and unsustainable. From the outset of BOP theory, multinational corporations have a key role to play: they can generate new sources of profit while seeking to meet the needs of these consumers in an innovative and sustainable way. The whole originality of this marketing approach resides in the fact that it is reinforced by social responsibility objectives. Hence corporations, after finding the right local partners (local government, local NGOs, small and medium-sized businesses) will be able to develop new products and services adapted to the poor.

Price affordability, social and environmental benefits are the keys to BOP which is designed to entice corporations to innovate in a sustainable and profitable way. One of the classic examples is that of Hindustan Lever Limited in India: by selling low-priced biodegradable soap in collaboration with local public health authorities, the company contributes to improving the hygiene of the poor without degrading the environment. The economic success is of course dependent on the volume of sales: given the low prices, this is the only way for corporations to make money. That is why BOP seems more suited to large national markets such as China or Brazil.

---

[50] Alongside Stuart Hart.
[51] UNDP 2017.

The BOP approach sounds quite promising: by fostering innovation, corporations may create economic value while responding to the needs of the world's poor in a responsible and sustainable way. Unfortunately, there is often a big gap between theory and practice: only in very few cases do corporations manage to generate a profit and develop new sustainable products. The social or environmental benefits are too easily forgotten for the sake of profits... Conversely, genuine sustainable BOP programs often end up being unprofitable.[52]

In any case, BOP did break new ground by insisting on the need for corporations to learn how to collaborate with local players, by pushing them to think of new ways of distributing and promoting their products and by urging them to put sustainability at the heart of their innovation policies.

To conclude, both the shared value and BOP concepts are innovative approaches aimed at embedding CSR into corporate strategies and operations. In a world currently dominated by liberal ideology, both of these concepts make sense. Despite their flaws, they have managed to push CSR beyond its traditional philanthropic vocation; in managerial terms, they have also brought practioners' attention to social responsibility issues in their management decisions and policies.

Yet, we feel that these approaches are at best transitory solutions to CSR embeddedness. We firmly believe in the inevitable emergence of a global political CSR approach, whereby corporations do their share in responding to our planet's pressing social and environmental issues beyond the traditional business-as-usual scenario. This, of course, can be achieved only if all actors in society play the game of deliberative democracy, each taking an active role in finding sustainable solutions for our unsustainable world. We will explore some of these impending issues in the following chapters.

Finally, today's CSR theoretical territory is more fragmented than ever. Multiple approaches coexist today: From liberal Friedmanites to shared value or BOP on the one hand, from ethics-based to corporate citizenship to political institutional approaches on the other, CSR theories

---

[52] For instance, French corporation Essilor selling low-price glasses to India's low income markets.

remain extremely diverse, spawned by moral, instrumental, utilitarian, political or sustainability-driven convictions.

Three main orientations seem to be emerging:

1) The *ethical orientation*, focused on doing good by giving back to the community, thus contributing to corporate image, reputation and legitimacy.

2) The *managerial orientation*, whereby CSR is seen as an operational response to a multitude of corporate issues, such as risk minimization, labor-related concerns, value maximization, etc.

3) The *political orientation*, when CSR becomes a strategic issue *per se*, i.e. when a firm acknowledges its role as provider of common good solutions, in addition to its business-as-usual priorities.

Whereas the ethical approach is the most widespread form of CSR, the managerial approach is clearly becoming more mainstream today. As for the political orientation, it has only just emerged, but is rapidly gaining ground among large corporations that have a long-term vision...

Another striking point is the deployment of CSR theories with regard to space. CSR was a strictly American concept up until the 1990s, but over the following decade, it had conquered Europe. Hybrid CSR approaches are emerging in the developing world and the concept continues to evolve. In fact, it may even be mutating.

Lastly, the question of the relationship between CSR and philanthropic practices across the world is more vital than ever: As embedded CSR discourses have been spreading across the corporate world, the reality often looks quite different. As my students have quite rightly observed, CSR all too often consists of charity-based philanthropic programs. The next section will help us understand how CSR can be embedded in operational reality.

2. Moving beyond philanthropy... For sure?

The first section enabled us to understand how CSR was born, how it developed and how diverse it has become today. Obviously, the U.S.-born philanthropy-based CSR has had a tremendous influence not only in the U.S., but also in many countries around the world where the traditional philanthropic practices have been renamed CSR in the last decade or so.

When one examines CSR practices around the world, it is clear that philanthropy is the most common "manifestation". In developing countries especially, a "giving back" approach of CSR remains predominant, being deep-rooted in the local cultural environment and most of the time related to the local religious practices (be it Christianity, Hinduism, Islam or Judaism, to name the largest denominations). In the U.S. itself, philanthropy remains the cornerstone of CSR policies and practices, being deeply embedded in the traditional Protestant ethic, as we could see it in the previous section.

Of course, one should not underestimate the fiscal attractiveness of philanthropic CSR for companies: If we look at developed countries, tax law is indeed very favorable to charity-based donations. For example, as charitable organizations, private foundations in the U.S. benefit from major tax exemptions. Even though they are not fully tax exempt like public foundations, the maximum they have to pay is set at 5% of their assets. In Europe, many countries, like the U.K. or France, also have very favorable laws for charitable organizations.

In India, where CSR remains by and large philanthropy-based, the recent Company Act from 2014 compels companies with annual revenues of more than 10 billion rupees (approximately 125 million euro or 160 million U.S. dollars) to dedicate 2% of their annual net profits to CSR activities. When one looks at the list of authorized CSR activities, the overwhelming majority appears to be charitable contributions to social development.

My students are thus quite right when associating CSR with donations and charity-based activities. The current reality does show a world where CSR is by and large synonymous with philanthropy. Yet, this world is changing fast: With globalization and the information revolution, society as a whole is demanding that companies adopt social responsibility measures that represent more than giving back to the community, all the more so as "philanthropic fiascoes" abound.

It is more and more commonly accepted that the business world does have its part to play in finding responses to the social and environmental challenges affecting our planet. Giving back is then viewed as a limited response: Only by making profound changes in the way they operate, produce and sell, will companies have a positive and long-lasting impact on people and the planet. This is also due to the inherent limits and flaws of philanthropic programs as we will see below.

This section intends to shed light on the various types of CSR responses that are currently undertaken by corporations. For this matter, we will rely on a three-stage pyramid we devised some time ago and which reflects many years of experience in the field. Since our aim is to move from theory to practice, concrete examples will be provided to illustrate our point.

2.1. The "CSR integration pyramid"

The pyramid shown below reflects the degree of integration of CSR into the company. It must be read from bottom to top, and it is widely assumed that reaching the top implies having fulfilled the previous two levels.

Three levels, or steps, have been identified: Philanthropy, compliance, and strategic CSR. Compared with Porter & Kramer's responsive vs strategic CSR diagram,[53] our pyramid definitely expresses a more European view.[54] Let us first describe each level.

Figure 6:   The CSR integration pyramid

---

[53] See previous section.
[54] We will explain this point below.

2.1.1. *Stage 1: Philanthropy*

Philanthropy is defined here by its traditional from, i.e. corporate dona-tions to charitable programs stemming either directly from the company or through its foundation. As was already mentioned, philanthropy is no doubt the most widespread form of CSR today, even though from a con-ceptual perspective it represents an early stage of CSR, as we saw it earlier.

Corporate philanthropic activities have existed for centuries in many parts of the world. Even though the concept is often associated with the U.S. due to the scale of philanthropic action in that country, it has been a traditional corporate practice in Latin America, the Middle East, India, Africa and many European countries for a long time. Its universal nature is due to its religious essence: All main world religions have a philan-thropic principle among their core values. Indeed, all religious codes stress the need to share success with the community and help those in need. This universality has enabled philanthropic practices to be carried out and understood almost everywhere on the planet. As was already men-tioned, fiscal benefits may also be associated with it. Finally, philanthropy is an easy way for a company to show compassion and care, and conse-quently gain a good image among the populations concerned.

Yet, philanthropy raises concern, as it quickly shows its limits. First, as clearly stressed by Porter & Kramer, philanthropic activities are often totally disconnected from the company's core operations and activities. Even more strikingly, philanthropy may be a way for the "worst in class" (companies with a very poor social and/or environmental record) to "buy" themselves a clean image in an easy, quick way. The figures show it: Among the biggest donors in the U.S. are many companies eager to offset their bad social and/or environmental reputation...[55]

In addition to being often disconnected from the core business of the company, philanthropy appears most of the time as a short-term practice, with many companies lacking consistency in the longer run. Companies eas-ily switch from one issue to another, from cultural heritage to biodiversity to

---

[55] For instance, a survey showed that the top 15 Fortune 500 Companies in the U.S. donated more than 100 million dollars in 2016. From "https://fortune.com/fortune500/".

social development or sports activities, to name a few. The actions and programs carried out all too often follow the desires or reflect the whims of some top personality, the President himself, or his/her spouse on the Foundation Board.[56]

Last but not least, philanthropy is still today merely viewed as *giving away*: Companies write a check, entrust their foundation with the use of the money, the foundation itself selects some NGOs to work with on the programs... What is important above all for the company is the fact of having donated the money to worthy causes. As to how the money is used, this is still rarely a priority, and remains the most negative aspect of philanthropy: Too much money ends up being poorly allocated. Corruption or embezzlement are not uncommon, and the money rarely ends up in the hands of the targeted population... One could — unfortunately — cite a myriad of examples from all around the world: Money given to indigenous communities being pocketed by one or two local "chiefs", unfinished hospitals or schools in Africa, money destined for slums never reaching its destination in Latin America... In addition, the programs are all too often managed in an "unprofessional" manner and the results are often quite unsatisfactory at the end of the day. In many countries unfortunately, not all NGOs are reliable partners.

This bleak picture does not mean that all philanthropic donations are inefficient and inconsistent! But one would be naïve not to recognize this state of facts. The main reason lies in the fact that traditional philanthropy is not viewed as *investment*. Ex post valuation protocols remain quite rare, and very few indicators are proposed to measure the efficiency level of a philanthropic program. From this perspective, some may argue that Milton Friedman was right in condemning CSR.

Nevertheless, philanthropy may serve a purpose for a company. Indeed, it contributes to linking the company with a given territory, enabling it to get rooted locally. Furthermore, it would not be commendable for a company not to support the local communities especially when these communities are poor and excluded. For multinational corporations operating far from their home base, it seems to be a

---

[56] The French have a typically French way of calling this practice: "The President's dancer" (*La danseuse du président*).

necessity in terms of image, legitimacy, and license to operate. This is not only from the point of view of the local populations, but also from that of local governments.

I once came across a very interesting case of a multinational company which had chosen to donate no money in a developing country where it had been operating for decades. This subsidiary from a multinational corporation held about 35% of the market along with a local family firm which had a similar market share, in a socially and environmentally sensitive industry. From the data I collected from interviews and secondary information, it appeared that the local family firm, "Firm A", had quite a positive image among the local community and national public opinion, giving back to the local community (hospitals, scholarships for family members, etc.), whereas the foreign subsidiary, "Firm B", had a very bad image and reputation. Even more tellingly, Firm A's safety record proved to be much better than Firm B's. Firm A had launched an internal advertising campaign on safety and had placated posters inside the premises showing real plant workers and their family with catchy slogans on safety compliance. On its side, firm B was merely complying with the safety guidelines sent in by the head office.

This case proved to be quite interesting and revealing: My key conclusions were that the refusal to donate by Firm B appeared to be a real obstacle in gaining recognition and understanding from the local population. Even the best safety measures from the head office proved to be inefficient due to the poor relations the firm had with its local territory. On the other hand, it seemed that workers were much more likely to "play the game" with Firm A because of the strong cultural ties and the mutual understanding.

Interestingly enough, many years after this research was conducted, Firm B decided to donate to the local stakeholders. Unsurprisingly, its safety record has improved dramatically, as proven by its latest sustainability report...

Even though it should not give way to generalizations, this case does show how important it is to give back to the community. The key is to find the right way of doing it, in order to avoid potential risks and pitfalls. The risk for the company of being entangled in corruption-related issues should of course never be underestimated.

To conclude, it seems that philanthropy may often be a nessary step in the social responsibility policy of a company. There are two key factors to make it efficient and successful: First, philanthropy has to become "strategic", i.e. more consistent with the company's activity, planned in the longer term and evaluated just like any other investment project. This is what Porter & Kramer advocate when talking about "strategic philanthropy". Second, let us remember that this is only Level 1 of CSR. Philanthropy may fulfill certain requirements, but in no case should it become the final objective of a CSR policy. If we consider that the company is a house, philanthropy is its garden...

The case for or against "strategic philanthropy"

As we saw in the previous chapter, Porter & Kramer in 2006 advocated for a radical transformation of traditional philanthropy so that philanthropic goals would be aligned with the company's general strategy. This so-called "strategic philanthropy" is based on the idea that by identifying untapped social needs companies may find ways of addressing them while gaining a competitite advantage and creating value.

One of the most convincing examples provided by Porter & Kramer is that of General Electric's (GE) *Healthymagination* Program launched in 2009 with the aim to provide better access and affordability to health care services. This for instance enabled GE to provide services in remote areas in Africa and Asia through the provision of innovative miniature medical equipments, such as ultrasound or MRIs. To reach this goal, the company invested massively in R&D, doubling its budget to reach 6 billion dollars and committing this amount for a period of over 6 years. Within a few years, the program allowed GE to generate profit while at the same time creating sustainable value for society.

This growing trend among multinationals generating new sources of income while meeting unmet social needs was coined as "shared value". Apart from the limits already discussed, it seems that only a few cases really prove convincing as of today. Thus, Mars' program *Visions4Change*, spanning over 30 years, is a rather impressive attempt by the multinational firm to sustain its supply of cocoa in the Cote d'Ivoire while bringing about long-lasting benefits to the cocoa-growers and their communities.

One major advantage in this case is the family structure of the Mars company making it easier to think long-term and integrate sustainability into the strategic vision. Yet, most of the shared value programs raise concerns about the triple bottom line approach, and especially the environmental sustainability dimension.

In the case of Mars, one of the major consequences is the increasing use of non-organic fertilizers among the Ivorian farmers. Other examples put forward by Porter & Kramer, such as Yara International, look even more controversial. Seen through a European lens, shared value programs seem to be focusing on community needs with environmental options that are more than questionable (GMOs, fertilizers, biotechnology). Finally, shared value, when implemented in the field, shows the limits of philanthropy being strategically embedded, since in the end the social benefits provided are limited, focused on key stakeholders like suppliers, and derive from the multinational's endless quest for new profit opportunities.

More generally speaking, the transformation of traditional philanthropy has been underway for a few decades, especially since famous philanthropists such as Bill Gates or Warren Buffet embarked on a strategic approach to philanthropy, for the sake of efficiency and impact.

Similarly, several philanthropy funds, such as Acumen, have been transforming themselves into "impact investment" funds. Indeed, while keeping a nonprofit legal status, the aim was to move way from donating and charities toward "investment strategies" with impact.

All these attempts to correct the mistakes of traditional philanthropy are noteworthy of course. Yet, the actual results are more often than not quite disappointing. The main reasons for this are the gap between the donors' good intentions and the reality in the field. Katherine Fulton, an expert in philanthropy, has experienced it all too often. As she says it quite bluntly:

> *"At its worst, strategic philanthropy can be a toxic mix of arrogance and ignorance, lacking critical understanding of the context, treating grantees not as partners but as mere instruments of a funder trying to meet a goal".*[57]

---

[57] Katherine Fulton, *The predicament of strategic philanthropy*, first published in *India Development Review*, January 30, 2018.

Once again, it seems that philanthropy *per se* has its limits. All the good intentions and the inherent morality put the emphasis on the donor's need to feel good, which rarely coincides with the actual needs of the targeted beneficiaries. Not to mention the sociological and cultural gaps!

As a European, my views on philanthropy are probably biased since we do not have the same cultural tradition on the old continent, especially in France, which is where I come from. Hence, I do not believe in strategic philanthropy as being an effective way of making companies genuinely responsible and sustainable. Yet, I also believe that philanthropy is an inevitable phenomenon, given its roots in many business cultures and its global appeal.

2.1.2. Stage 2: Compliance

Moving beyond philanthropy, companies start to internalize CSR into their activities and operations by engaging in a "compliance" approach. Compliance here should be understood as a reactive attitude based on the understanding that for various reasons companies are required to adopt a set of practices, norms and standards to "comply" with rising expectations around social responsibility issues. By no means does compliance in this case refer to strict legal rules or regulations. It has to be understood as a soft conformity-driven attitude.

The compliance stage is thus characterized by a responsive approach one could equate with "we, as a company, have to": we have to meet the expectations of society on a certain number of CSR issues. "We" have to show our willingness to take into account social pressures urging us to minimize our negative impacts on society and/or the environment.[58]

These social pressures may come from a variety of stakeholders: Customers, public authorities, competitors, or society at large. In developed societies for instance, customers are pushing companies to propose products with greater social or environmental benefits. Thus, more and more companies will seek labels that reflect their efforts in greening their products or taking better account of workplace or human rights issues. Public regulators, especially in the European Union and in some other

---

[58] In this case, our compliance approach is quite similar to Porter & Kramer's responsive CSR based on "mitigating harm from value chain activities".

developed countries (including some States, like California) are imposing stricter and stricter rules on waste management, resource use, or energy efficiency. In this case, companies are bound to adopt a compliance attitude by anticipating new legislations in these areas.

Competitors may also push companies to adopt a compliance attitude, through benchmarking and institutional mimetism. When a company is a leader in CSR in a given industry, competitors tend to realize how important it becomes to adopt better standards so as to conform to new industry practices. For instance, when French cement multinational Lafarge entered the Mexican market in the 1990s, the local giant Cemex quickly realized it would have to develop its CSR beyond traditional philanthropy in order to face the new competition from the French company, then considered to be a forerunner in CSR and sustainability.[59]

More generally speaking, society at large keeps asking businesses for improved social or environmental practices. And the media is often ready to amplify these demands. The exponential acceleration of information that flows around the planet no doubt contributes.

This compliance approach took a new turn about twenty years ago. Indeed, as we saw it in the previous chapter, the emergence of non-U.S. CSR approaches in the 1990s coincides with the growing awareness around sustainability. Faced with mounting external institutional pressures, Western European companies started to introduce CSR policies which clearly departed from traditional philanthropic activities.

By recognizing that they had some degree of responsibility to endorse regarding social and environmental issues affecting the planet, Western European multinationals along with a few North American and Japanese multinationals started to launch international initiatives aimed at integrating CSR to their business agendas. This took the form of multi-stakeholder initiatives, such as the WBCSD created in 1995 by several large multinational companies or the *Global Reporting Initiative* launched in 1997 by non-profit organization CERES and which has become the internationally recognized reporting standard for sustainability.

---

[59] Since that time, the company has unfortunately been confronted with several scandals, among which was a highly unethical case in Syria.

Taking advantage of this new trend which was often nicknamed the "market of virtue", other actors such as consultancies or private standardization agencies designed innovative standards and norms which could help multinationals set up socially responsible processes in their operations and activities. Thus appeared new ISO standards related to environmental management (the ISO 14001 series in 1996, revised in 2004 and 2015) and other private standards related to work conditions (the multistakeholder Social Accountability SA 8000 in 1997, the British standard OHSAS 18001 in 1999, to name a few).

In addition, international institutions themselves started to endorse social responsibility objectives. The U.N. developed the *Global Compact* in 2000, the *OECD guidelines for multinational enterprises* were drafted in the 1980s, then in 1991, to be revised in 2001 and 2011, covering responsible business conduct issues more and more extensively. To these iniatives may be added all the labels which were launched for eco-products, fair-trade programs, industry certifications, etc. All in all, multinationals at the time gradually adopted some sort of compliance approach toward CSR.

More recently in 2010, and after years of lenghty rounds of discussions, ISO launched the first-ever standard on social responsibility, ISO 26000, which, while being a non-certifiable standard, offers companies around the world a comprehensive CSR framework document, which is to be viewed as a tool for progress.

Compliance may also be triggered by a social or environmental crisis a company has had to cope with. The acceleration of media pressure and impact is clearly adding momentum: Companies are more than ever under the spotlight when caught within a scandal or crisis. From the Deepwater Horizon oil spill in 2010 to the Rana Plaza collapse in 2013, from contaminated food to forced or child labor, businesses are summoned by society to provide new and adequate responses. This is of course especially the case for multinational brands with a broad public impact.

Whereas this compliance attitude developed mostly in the developed world first, a similar movement has been observed among developing countries companies over the last few years. Indeed, the globalization of value chains, the growing interdepency among national economies have contributed to the spread of CSR issues. For a growing number of small and medium sized businesses in the developing world today, adopting CSR practices means gaining access to the international market. Bound by their own CSR engagements, multinationals are increasingly putting pressure on their suppliers and subcontractors, and require that they in turn start adopting and implementing some of their key CSR objectives.

For instance, it has become commonplace in many international contracts to require suppliers or subcontractors to be ISO 14001 certified. Moreover, the growing number of social or environmental audits performed by international clients is having direct consequences on local business practices, pushing the latter to find ways of minimizing some of their negative impacts.

Thus, compliance appears as a necessary step in the internalization of CSR. The wide range of tools at disposal makes it easier for companies to adopt them; furthermore, the generalization of such practices is mainstreaming CSR around the world: Companies do more and more naturally understand the necessity of and their interest in adopting such practices. In a nutshell, adopting a compliance approach to CSR helps companies enhance on the one hand their reputation and image, and when faced with crises or scandals, their legitimacy, i.e. their license to operate.[60]

Nevertheless, this compliance approach has its limits. First, its efficiency widely varies, and this is due to the nature itself of the compliance tools at disposal. Most of these standards, guidelines and labels are indeed soft law instruments, i.e. privately engineered initiatives which have no strict binding force compared to the traditional hard law instruments. The advantage for companies is their flexibility — the fact that they are incentives rather than legal obligations. The main weaknesses lie in their nature itself: they may become mere P.R. tools once companies have understood that they do not risk much resorting to them...

This soft law phenomenon is clealy linked to the growing influence of CSR around the world and to the need to find alternatives to legislations which often prove their lack of efficiency, or even more, their irrelevance in a context of globalization. The debate over hard vs soft law is a never-ending one.[61]

---

[60] See above. Porter & Kramer 2006.
[61] See Chapter 3.

Let us just say at this point that soft law has had a tremendous impact in the engagement of companies into compliance-based CSR. Let us also add that many of these soft law instruments are increasingly becoming "harder", even giving way to new legislation in some countries.

As a result, compliance appears to be a crucial stage in the adoption of CSR policies but with a highly varying degree of impact and efficiency. It is clearly the most common type of CSR once a company starts moving beyond philanthropy and adopts new tools and processes aiming at putting social responsibility issues on the corporate agenda. But its concrete implementation may take very diverse forms: From very strict rules and processes to mere communication-based initiatives, including real improvements on some managerial and business-related aspects.

After observing companies around the world, one may distinguish between three main types of compliance: Low level, medium level and high level compliance. Or to put it differently, from soft to strict compliance. Thus, many developing countries are presently moving into compliance-based CSR, so that they are generally found between low and medium level CSR. One of the main reasons for this is the usually poorer level of external institutional pressure: Their main driver for compliance-based CSR remains institutional exposure and access to market.

European companies due to the institutional context are usually found between medium and high level compliance. In some countries, like Germany, multinationals have typically adopted a strict compliance approach to CSR which may be largely explained by the strict regulatory tradition in the country. Many managers I talked to in developing countries (Middle East and North Africa in this case) made a clear distinction between social or environmental audits performed by German companies versus those performed by other multinationals. For the former, recommendations from the client company needed to be clearly taken into account and followed, for the latter, there always remained room for discussion... To some extent, the same seems to be the case in Asia where Japanese companies are usually known for their strict application of the rules.

When it comes to U.S. companies, this compliance stage appears to be a little less relevant than in Europe, given the lower level of institutional pressure. For sure, many U.S. multinationals have adopted CSR instruments, but tend to favor the softest of these instruments. Other factors such as the type of industry or the markets these companies operate in clearly play a decisive role. But most U.S. companies follow by and large the pattern devised by Porter & Kramer in 2006: They are likely to adopt a compliance approach to CSR if they see an economical gain in it or if they are bound to it by their stakeholders. Otherwise, CSR remains philanthropy-grounded, hence the move for some of them towards "strategic philanthropy".[62]

2.1.3. *Stage 3: Strategic CSR*

The ultimate step in CSR integration is the "strategic" phase. "Strategic" here means that some key social and/or environmental issues have clearly been identified by top management and are being aligned with the overall strategy. More often than not, companies move into this stage when a new vision for the next ten years is being developed, which is currently the case for many multinational companies. In this case, some key CSR issues get embedded into corporate strategy, leading to further embeddedness into operational activities. With this strategic approach to CSR, companies are reaching the much-needed convergence between CSR and business priorities, more than 60 years after Bowen's seminal inspiration.

The strategic embeddedness of CSR is a new phenomenon: If one sets aside some "champions" that have CSR values at their core (such as the Anglo-Saxon pioneers The Body Shop, Ben & Jerry's or Patagonia) and a few early adopters,[63] strategic embeddedness has been emerging over the last five years, mostly among Western European and U.S. multinationals, in some specific industries such as consumer goods (foodstuffs, personal care, garment and footwear) or high impact manufacturing (construction).

For sure, the line between high-level compliance and strategic CSR is not that clear. Yet, one of the main differences lies in the impulses of top management, and especially the CEO. Virtually all cases of strategic embeddedness are characterized by a strong personal commitment from the company CEO; this is required especially to convince top management and shareholders of the relevance to integrate CSR values into the overall

---

[62] See above.

[63] See for instance the case of *Interface* illustrated in Chapter 5.

strategy of the company. These CEOs may also act as spokespeople for the media and other external stakeholders. To take a few current examples, one can mention Indra Nooyi[64] (Pepsico), Paul Polman (Unilever) or Emmanuel Faber (Danone) who have been steering their companies towards sustainability-led CSR over the past few years.

It goes without saying that management impulse is necessary but not sufficient: A clear strategic plan emanating from the top needs to be accompanied by changes in organizational and managerial processes, from adopting new key performance indicators to efficient and comprehensive data collection processes, as well as appropriate performance goals and incentives for all staff, geared to their own functions and responsibilities. In addition, cross-functional coordination is crucial, along with bottom up processes whereby operational staff may discuss and consult with management on a fluid basis.

In this respect, the designation (preferably on a voluntary basis) by more and more companies of "champions" or "ambassadors", i.e. staff members who willingly agree to share and diffuse CSR practices around them, seems highly beneficial. It goes without saying that this cannot replace appropriate training for employees and internal communication devices.

This first type of strategic CSR is clearly based on a value chain approach, as Porter & Kramer identified it. One observes today more and more multinational companies adopting this approach since it enables them to move toward implementing a triple bottom line approach. Strategic CSR is clearly sustainability-driven, with a strong focus on the environmental dimension. Driven by an inspirational long-term vision, such a CSR policy based on the value chain pushes companies to first work on the materiality of their CSR issues and then adopt a comprehensive, systematic and measurable approach to CSR. The review and reporting stage is of course crucial and remains one of the main challenges to date.

Among companies having adopted a strategic approach, one may cite Unilever, Danone, L'Oréal, Puma or Pepsico. They are of course just a few today. Below is a table summarizing some key features regarding their CSR and sustainability commitments.

---

[64] "CEO until the end of 2018"; and for Paul Polman: CEO until the end of 2018, Polman has just founded a consultancy "Imagine" whose objective is to contribute to meeting the sustainable development objectives.

Table 1:   Some examples of strategic CSR deployment

DANONE	Set up in 2001, the *Danone way* is a self-assessment tool used in all business units. Its aim is to promote best practices in sustainable development. Every year, all subsidiaries conduct a self-assessment which is then reviewed by headquarters, which then updates sustainability performance objectives. Furthermore, as of today, around 1,500 managers have a substantial part of their annual bonuses (about one-third) based on sustainability objectives. Danone is also known for having been a pioneer in launching innovative social businesses.
UNILEVER	The Unilever *Sustainable Living Plan* (USLP) is the Dutch company's strategic plan for CSR. As the company stated it, the aim is to "achieve our vision to grow our business, whilst decoupling our environmental footprint from our growth and increasing our positive social impact". The Plan has set social, health-related and environmental targets for 2020 and 2030, which are reviewed every year in the progress report. This top-down policy was strongly supported by CEO Paul Polman. It aims at bringing about deep changes in product development and brand strategies.
L'ORÉAL	The French company launched in 2013 its "sharing beauty with all" sustainability commitment program with clear quantified targets for 2020. This applies to all business units, and along the entire value chain. A strong focus is placed on the crucial R&D phase.
PUMA	The German footwear company is known for its ambitious suppliers' policy. Working with its key strategic suppliers in a collaborative way, Puma aims at long-term cooperation with them so as to co-create socially responsible supply chains. An example is the exclusive relationship Puma had for year with South-African textile manufacturer Impahla Clothing. By helping them enhance social and environmental standards, the German company definitely contributed to Impahla's impressive value creation and growth, leading to the design of exclusive Sub-Saharan brands BLK and Linebreak. From being a supplier of multinationals, the South African company has now suceeded in launching its own line of upmarket sportswear!
PEPSICO	Following the will of its Indian female CEO Indra Nooyi (up until 2018), the U.S. multinational launched its Performance with Purpose plan in 2006. Quoting Ms Nooyi in 2017: "Today, we're more dedicated to Performance with Purpose than ever before and we're harnessing the power of our global scale to drive meaningful change across countries and continents. We are all in. Sustainability is who we are, it's what fuels our business, and it's why I believe PepsiCo's best days are yet to come." With targets set for 2025, the company has embarked on an ambitious journey with many challenges ahead.

Needless to say, deploying strategic CSR is far from easy: Many contradictions and obstacles lie ahead. First, it remains quite challenging for companies to align their CSR commitments to their overall strategies, all the more so when in a context of fierce global competition and financial profitability pressures. Second, whereas the top-down impulse is crucial, the implementation process across products and countries remains difficult.

The examples given above should in no way be interpreted as perfect CSR cases. Challenges abound: How can Danone keep pushing its efforts in a higly competitive industry with new potential market shares around the world? Will L'Oréal manage to get customer approval in their ambitious product transformations? How can Unilever deploy its plan effectively given the complexity and diversity of its product range? How do you convince marketing teams that this is the best strategy to enhance sales in the future? (this applies to all!). Can Pepsico reasonably insist on its sustainability ambitions while keeping selling products which for most of them are not sustainable to people's health? These are just some of the questions that may be addressed to these multinationals. But while no one knows what the outcome will be in a few years from now, it is clear that change from the top is underway...

For this top-down impulse to gain momentum inside the company, organizational change is required, mindset revolutions are needed. As often observed, one of the hardest challenges is to convince middle managers to play the game. More often than not, middle management teams are quite reluctant to risk changing business as usual practices. This is especially the case in marketing departments where CSR and sustainability are still too often viewed as a narrow niche market which will never generate significant sales. R&D is also critical in the sense that engineering cultures may be deep rooted in traditional beliefs making it very hard to shift to organic-based innovations.

In other big-impact industries such as energy and construction, many multinationals (for instance, Engie, Veolia or Vattenfall) are currently struggling to embed sustainability in their strategic visions. Pushed by the E.U. strategy aimed to decarbonize the energy mix, these companies are currently adopting innovative strategies to embed new socially responsible and sustainable practices into their core businesses.

This can take the form of internal innovative labs, external acquisitions of greentech/cleantech startups or funds set up by the company with an aim to invest in equity in promising energy start-ups (like for example Engie's *Rassembleurs d'énergies* Fund). This new trend is a promising evolution for CSR embeddedness. In most cases, the CSR department acts as a catalyst, prompting the company to learn how to have more sustainable products and operations by acquiring new competences. Even oil and gas companies are acquiring greentech or cleantech to diversify and green their portfolios (French company Total acquiring green consultancy Greenflex for instance).

As we could see from the previous examples, strategic CSR is definitely sustainability-driven. Sustainability with its triple bottom line approach is a powerful integration strategy that operates a linkage between former externalities and corporate performance. In this respect, the 17 U.N. SDGs (sustainable development goals) launched in 2015[65] may be a powerful engine. Let us just hope that companies will use them as strategic tools and not P.R. icons... Scrutinizing corporate behavior towards the SDGs will thus be crucial!

At the end of the day, value-chain based strategic CSR definitely requires a convergence of factors: strong impulse from the top, ongoing commitment from the staff, as well as consistent and efficient processes and measurement systems. Even though this trend is quite recent, i.e. a few years, our observations tend to show that the willingness to move toward strategically embedding CSR is gaining momentum today. Our assumption is that whatever the obstacles lying ahead, this trend is irreversible. For the sake of the planet, let us hope so!

This introductory chapter enabled us to understand how the concept of CSR emerged and gradually branched out into many different schools and approaches. It is indeed relevant to go back to the roots of CSR to measure the importance of philanthropy and ethics as foundational pillars of CSR.

With the 1990s and the emergence of a European school of thought on CSR appeared new forms of CSR, institutionally embedded and sustainability driven. This European approach finds its concrete

---

[65] See Introduction.

implementation today in the value-chain driven strategic CSR policies put in place by more and more European multinationals. On the other hand, the U.S. historic CSR is gradually evolving into strategic philanthropy and shared value approaches.

Besides, the globalization process is having a strong impact on CSR, bringing about a globalization of compliance-based CSR policies through a series of internationally recognized tools and instruments. As a consequence, this gradually cascades down to global supply chains, embarking thousands of businesses around the world which in turn are moving toward compliance-based CSR.

All in all, traditional philanthropy, while remaining in many cases the bedrock of CSR practices worldwide is being rethought and redesigned, being supplemented by compliance-driven CSR practices. More and more in the developing world, CSR today means more than give back to the community. CSR is gradually being internalized and/or aligned with the business objectives of the firms.

Finally, globalization also leads to a hybridization process, especially in the developing world (such as in India). It is besides noticeable that a major part of the most recent CSR literature is focusing both on global value chains and on CSR in developing countries.

In this respect, it will be interesting to see how efficient the 17 Sustainable Development Goals will be in harmonizing CSR approaches around the world, embedding them into strategic objectives, and building up new convergences between businesses, public authorities and the civil societies.

CHAPTER 2

THE STAKEHOLDER CHALLENGE

One of the very first concepts that come to mind when considering CSR is that of the "stakeholders". The term, coined in the 1980s, has become a buzzword today, not only in the field of CSR, but more generally in management and political sciences. It generally refers to all the categories of people who are involved in and affected by an organization.

This chapter seeks first to examine how the concept came into being, what it means from a theoretical standpoint and what the main limitations are, especially from a non-U.S. perspective. We will then focus on the concrete implementation of stakeholder management with a view to going beyond the usual rhetoric about stakeholder inclusiveness in various CSR approaches. Indeed, it seems that "walking the talk" in terms of stakeholder management remains a very tricky issue. Everybody keeps talking about stakeholders, yet for most businesses, they are far from being a priority. We will then try to put forward some innovative practices in the field, whereby businesses do actually take their stakeholders into account when making strategic decision pertaining to social and environmental issues.

1. The birth of a concept

Although the term "stakeholder" officially appeared in the 1980s[1] in the U.S., the notion of stakeholder had already been implicitly present for several decades. Indeed, whereas the 1920s and 30s saw many debates over whether companies ought to systematically favor stockholders' versus society's interests,[2] the post-war years brought about a renewed interest in business responsibilities toward society. As we saw in the first chapter, some prominent business leaders started to call for an *"equitable balance between the interest of various interest groups"*.[3] The groundbreaking Johnson & Johnson *Credo* written in 1943 clearly stated that the company was accountable to several categories of people directly related to its activity.

This renewed interest in the societal impact of business was due to several factors among which the rise of mega-corporations and a mature consumer society in the country, the growing influence of labor unions as well as the emergence of modern management education. This of course coincides with the official birth of the CSR concept with Bowen's seminal book. Even though Bowen himself did not explicitly develop the concept of "stakeholders", he did insist on the need to create "Industry Councils" on which would sit independent members: This was clearly a way of acknowledging the need for non-stockholder representation in the management of the firm.

In other words, the notion of "interested groups" seems to have been inherent in the development of modern business theory in the U.S. as a counterpart to the dominant stockholders' view, opposing the proponents of a purely liberal view of the firm to those stressing the societal involvement of businesses. More profoundly, this debate has been paramount in the U.S. since the advent of modern businesses, revolving around the role and mission of businesses toward society. As we saw in the previous chapter, this fundamental issue was raised as early as the end of the XIXth century and has remained critical ever since. Indeed, should businesses concentrate all

---

[1] The term first appeared in a 1963 Internal Memorandum of the Stanford Research Institute (in Freeman & Reed, 1983).
[2] See Chapter 1, Dodge vs Ford Court decision, Berle & Means, 1932.
[3] Frank Abrams, 1951.

their efforts on satisfying the owners, i.e. the stockholders, or should they, on the contrary, take into account the various demands and expectations of key categories of people who are in direct relation with them?

1.1. *The foundations*

The fact that the term "stakeholder" officially appeared in the 1980s comes as no surprise. It corresponded to a strong reaction at the time of the academic community against the neo-conservative Friedmanite view which prevailed not only in academic circles but also within the Federal Government (the Reagan era). The concept was indeed popularized by an academic, R. Edward Freeman who, in 1984, published a landmark book,

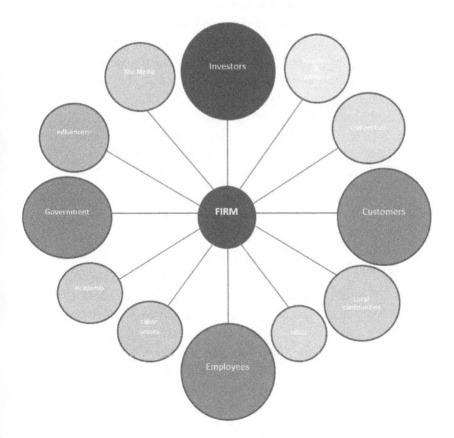

Figure 7: The Stakeholder model

Strategic Management — A stakeholder approach. In his book, Freeman defined and developed the stakeholder model, attempting to provide some concrete approaches for businesses wishing to integrate stakeholders into their policies. Freeman's book may be viewed as a response to Porter's value chain model and the agency theory, yet it also offers potential solutions to strategic management dilemmas and justifies the rise of business ethics in the U.S.

The original definition was quite straightforward: stakeholders were defined by Freeman as "*any group or individual who can affect or is affected by the achievement of the organization's objectives*". With this definition, Freeman clearly displayed a utilitarian and instrumental vision of stakeholder management, since stakeholder demands are relevant only to the extent that they meet the firm's objectives.

This led to a well-publicized model in which the firm is the focal entity connected unilaterally to a certain number of stakeholder groups, whose number usually varies between 8 and 12. It is, of course, important to remember that the stakeholder concept is centered around the firm and clearly reflects a *managerial* view of the world. Today, the term stakeholder is also used in other contexts where there is no such firm-centric approach.

Below is a summary table describing the key expectations from major stakeholders regarding CSR issues. These issues will of course be further developed in the following chapters.

Stakeholders	Key Expectations
Employees	Employees are key stakeholders who are likely to expect the firm to provide a positive social contribution beyond the traditional Human Resources (HR) agenda. Depending on the extent of the HR policy set in place, typical issues may include health and safety, well-being at work or long-term personal development in the company. More and more employees also expect their firm to engage in social and environmental commitments. Such commitments may contribute to the firm's attractiveness, as is increasingly the case in developed countries. As a matter of fact, more and more companies promote their CSR during their recruitment processes.

(Continued)

(*Continued*)

Stakeholders	Key Expectations
Clients/ customers	Clients and customers are certainly becoming more and more sensitive to the social and environmental benefits provided by a company's products or services. This is striking in European countries and some U.S. states, such as California. Companies are expected by these "CSR-conscious" consumers to provide transparent information about their supply chains and production processes. More generally, customers now expect fair and reliable information from companies.
Shareholders/ investors	Even though investors and shareholders are focused on the financial returns they can reap, an increasing number of institutional shareholders are requiring that companies in which they invest take into account some key CSR issues like climate change. Such is the case for major oil and gas companies being challenged by the most powerful pension funds such as CalPERS or the New York State Employees Fund.
Partners/ suppliers	The case of suppliers and business partners is quite peculiar: Indeed, more and more suppliers and subcontractors are being pressured by client companies to comply with their CSR requirements. Conversely, these stakeholders expect the client firms to engage in long-term trust-based relationships.
Government	Government (including all levels of public authority) is an ambivalent stakeholder. Depending on the institutional context, it may be anything from a silent stakeholder to an extremely influential one, especially when it starts pushing a social and/or environmental agenda. Government pressure may become particularly strong. Such is the case in the E.U. and California. In the developing world, governments are demanding more and more that businesses take up social and environmental issues and be the drivers for change and progress in those countries. Such is the case of India for instance.

(*Continued*)

(Continued)

Stakeholders	Key Expectations
Local communities	Local communities are key stakeholders on CSR issues, due to the direct impact of businesses on territories. In developing countries especially, communities are expecting companies to contribute to their development. This has mostly been done so far through philanthropic programs, not to mention the easy way out, "hush money",[4] practiced especially in big impact industries such as extractive industries. Today, as the limits of traditional philanthropy are increasingly apparent, some businesses are considering other ways of contributing to local communities. Strategic philanthropy or social businesses are being developed in many parts of the world.
NGOs	Non Governmental Organizations (NGOs) are extremely influential when it comes to CSR since their *raison d'être* is to advocate and champion CSR causes. Yet, the world of NGOs is infinitely complex. While many NGOs are keen to partner with businesses for financial reasons, other NGOs represent the firm's worst enemies since their mission is to attack businesses by denouncing all their wrongdoings. Caught in the middle, many NGOs can be both partners and enemies.
Media	The media can be a highly influential stakeholder, especially for brands. Indeed, brands need the media to communicate their values to the general public. At the same time, everybody knows now about the risks of greenwashing. For the media, greenwashing is a practice they are keen to denounce, first because they consider this vilification to be part of their mission, second because it pays off… Thus, firms need to learn how to engage in long-term trust-based relationships with the media.

(Continued)

---

[4]Literally money given to communities to silence them.

(Continued)

Stakeholders	Key Expectations
Competitors	As indirect stakeholders, competitors are important to firms since they may provide them with insights into best practices in the field. Benchmarking is indeed highly important for players in the same industry. Besides, competitors may also sometimes turn out to be partners and allies: This is the case when several players from the same industry pool their resources to work out industry-wide standards or join forces in R&D to develop new packagings (such as is the case of the cosmetics industry in France where several cutting edge projects involve cooperation among competitors).
Influencers	In a world of social media and constant connectivity, influencers, such as celebrities or bloggers may play a crucial role in promoting CSR actions. For example, the successful launch of the Toyota Prius in the U.S. was largely due to the boost given by Hollywood celebrities such as Leonardo DiCaprio.
Academics	The academic world is also an important stakeholder today since it is eager to collaborate with businesses in order to provide them with research expertise and help them design and develop environmental and/or social innovations. The academic world can also be a critical analyst, especially in regards to CSR experts in management and social sciences.

Whereas some experts and academics include the environment at large or animal species as stakeholders, we refrain from doing so since stakeholders must be in a position to have their representatives deal directly with the firm. This is not the case for the natural environment or animal species which, in this case, are best represented by NGOs. Some today advocate as an alternative to always leave an empty chair during meetings, this empty chair "representing" the natural environment...

Freeman's model and the emergence of the stakeholder concept led to a plethora of books, articles and conferences which provided a blurred and often contradictory theoretical framework.[5] Stakeholders were soon categorized, such as internal vs external stakeholders. Internal stakeholders such as staff members, management, and shareholders operate within the company, as opposed to consumers, regulators, suppliers and local communities who are external to firms.

The other well-known distinction was established between primary and secondary stakeholders.[6] Primary stakeholders were defined as those having a direct stake in the company such as staff, clients, strategic partners and shareholders vs external stakeholders such as government, media, NGOs or competitors exerting an influence and having a potential impact on the company's reputation.

1.2. *Toward a normative theory?*

In the 1990s, academic research made two interesting attempts at synthesizing and unifying the stakeholder management literature: In their 1995 paper, Donaldson & Preston analyzed the abundant body of literature on stakeholders to provide a classification of stakeholder theory according to three main dimensions: Descriptive accuracy, instrumental power and normative validity. They first identified a descriptive approach, which *"describes the corporation as a constellation of cooperative and competitive interests possessing intrinsic value"*.[7] Although they confirmed its relevance, Donaldson & Preston concluded that the descriptive approach did not have any managerial implications, its mere contribution being to provide a more accurate view of the reality of the firm as opposed to the shareholder view based on the powerful but simplistic agency theory. They then discussed the instrumental approach which *"establishes a framework for examining the connections, if any, between the practice of stakeholder management and the achievement*

---

[5]Donaldson, T. & Preston, L.E.: "The Stakeholder Theory of the Corporation: Concepts, Evidence, and Implications", *The Academy of Management Review*, 20(1), pp. 65–91.

[6]See for instance Clarkson, 1995 or Bucholtz & Carroll, 2012.

[7]Donaldson & Preston, p. 66.

of various corporate performance goals".[8] After careful scrutiny, they argued that the managerial implications were clear in theory but not easily applicable or measurable in reality. The multiplicity of stakeholders and the complexity of their demands make it extremely difficult to establish a correlation between managing stakeholders and enhancing corporate performance.

Finally, after showing that all three dimensions were interrelated, Donaldson & Preston placed the normative approach at the core, identifying two key aspects of it:

"Although Theses 1 and 2 are significant aspects of the stakeholder theory, its fundamental basis is normative and involves acceptance of the following ideas: (a) Stakeholders are persons or groups with legitimate interests in procedural and/or substantive aspects of corporate activity. Stakeholders are identified by their interests in the corporation, whether the corporation has any corresponding functional interest in them. (b) The interests of all stakeholders are of intrinsic value. That is, each group of stakeholders merits consideration for its own sake and not merely because of its ability to further the interests of some other group, such as the shareowners".[9]

Interestingly enough, Donaldson & Preston based their conclusions on the fact that the normative approach was the most relevant one, considering potential managerial implications. Indeed, if one considers the property rights theory, developing a normative theory of stakeholder management is more relevant and ethical than the dominant shareholder value approach.[10]

"The plain truth is that the most prominent alternative to the stakeholder theory (i.e., the "management serving the shareowners" theory) is morally untenable. The theory of property rights, which is commonly supposed to support the conventional view, in fact — in its modern and pluralistic form-supports the stakeholder theory instead".[11]

---

[8] *Ibid.*, p. 67.
[9] *Ibid.*
[10] The corporate governance issues will be addressed in Chapter 6.
[11] *Op. Cit.*, pp. 87–88.

The key contribution of Donaldson & Preston was no doubt to stress the normative potential of the stakeholder theory. In doing so, they participated in the rising corporate governance debate. As we will see later, the stakeholder view of the firm is beginning to be recognized by law in several countries today. Even though it may not be directly linked to the property rights issue as they had ascertained, the idea that a firm is accountable not only to its shareholders but also to its stakeholders is clearly gaining ground.

A relevant example of this evolution is illustrated by the creation of the B-Corp status in the U.S. Present today in more than 35 States, this legal certification requires companies by law to have a dual obligation: Besides being accountable financially to its shareholders, the company is also accountable to its stakeholders through its obligation to publish a social and environmental report along with the annual financial report. Its shareholders must also agree on the social/environmental purpose of the firm, which has an impact on the dividends they may expect. The most famous companies with this certification today are the U.S. clothing company Patagonia and Danone North America.

In their other contributions, Donaldson & Preston insisted on the fact that the stakeholder theory was purely managerial in essence, and that its efficiency needed to be tested and proven. The practical dimension of the theory is clearly explained in the following excerpt:

> *"Stakeholder management requires, as its key attribute, simultaneous attention to the legitimate interests of all appropriate stakeholders, both in the establishment of organizational structures and general policies and in case-by-case decision making".*

This is where the limits of the theory become obvious. Indeed, how can managers pay *"simultaneous attention to the legitimate interests of all appropriate shareholders?"* Furthermore, how can managers determine what the "legitimate" interests of the stakeholders are and who the "appropriate" stakeholders are?

1.3. Prioritizing stakeholders?

Subsequent research attempted to respond to this question by providing models that enabled the prioritization of stakeholders. One of the most relevant attempts is that of Mitchell *et al.* who, in 1997, designed a typology that identified stakeholders according to three main variables: Power, legitimacy and urgency, with a view to assessing their salience to the firm's managers. According to Mitchell *et al.*, the definitive stakeholder possesses all three attributes. Today, many mapping tools designed to help companies categorize and prioritize their stakeholders are available.

However, many questions remain: On what grounds will the firms determine the power, legitimacy or urgency of their stakeholders? When and how does one decide that a stakeholder has changed categories? More importantly, the whole process is controlled by the firm, since the stakeholder theory's postulate is that the firm is the sole initiator of the CSR agenda. This means that the firm will always consider the stakeholders from its own perspective, according to its own interests, and not according to the interests of the stakeholder themselves.

This then may lead to major ethical dilemmas. To take but a few examples, how will the firm consider the interests of its employees while constantly striving to increase its performance and profits? How will the firm find the right response to media pressure? How will it be able to understand the long-term interests of the local communities? How will it communicate to the consumers?

1.4. The conceptual limits of stakeholder theory

Actually, when looking at the complexities and intricacies of the stakeholder management models that have been proposed over the last 30 years, one realizes just how fundamentally Anglo-Saxon stakeholder theory actually is.

Firstly, whatever the variations proposed, the underlying assumption is that the firm's responsibility is defined by a series or tacit contractual agreements conducted with its stakeholders as diverse as employees, public authorities, NGOs and suppliers. As we saw previously, the liberal-contractualist conception predominates in U.S.-style CSR. In the case of stakeholder theory, the contractualist view prevails, clearly opposed to the strict Friedmanite profit-maximization view of the firm. On the other hand, however, it constitutes a managerial theory which remains within a non-political regulation-based environment.

This is where the continental European school of CSR is most critical of the stakeholder approach. True, this theory provided a counter model to the shareholder view of the firm, thus pushing companies to take into account other interests besides the financial expectations of their shareholders.

Yet, the inherent limits of the theory's applicability are due to its very nature: The proposed contractualist approach is very ill-suited to the European environment where the firm is much more embedded in an institutional framework. This brings us back to Matten & Moon's implicit vs explicit types of CSR.[12] Stakeholder theory clearly provides an explicit view of CSR whereby the firm itself sets social responsibility objectives. Thus, taking into account the interests of various stakeholders is part of the explicit CSR mission of the firm toward society.

Conversely, the European approach is largely implicit since firms are embedded within powerful institutional mechanisms. The question of labor unions is a case in point; indeed, in continental Europe social dialogue with the unions is a fundamental legal mechanism that governs labor relations. Unsurprisingly, stakeholder theory does not consider this question: as shown by several European authors,[13] labor unions are not even mentioned as stakeholders in the classic models. German author Preuss coined the term "stake-seekers" for labor unions, meaning that they had not yet been granted stakeholder status, but were to obtain it. He went so far as to state that stakeholder theory was un-European. We will elaborate on the question of CSR and social dialogue in the following chapter, since it has obviously remained a "blind spot" in CSR/stakeholder theory thus far.

The main critique has come from the Francophone school of CSR. For several authors, the stakeholder theory depicts a society which is governed solely by private interests and demands. Not only does the theory position the firm as the central actor, but it also bases managerial decisions on tacit bilateral contracts with various stakeholders taken individually. Stakeholder theory is based on an ahistorical conception of society in which collective views have been suppressed. As a result, stakeholder theory fosters a privatization process of society.[14]

---

[12] See Chapter 1.

[13] See for instance, Preuss, 2008, and Delbard, 2009.

[14] See for instance the works of Cazal and/or Pesqueux.

These arguments are especially valid in a non-U.S. context: They highlight a key issue which has been largely ignored by mainstream CSR literature, namely the link between CSR and regulation. This ambiguity manifests itself in the European definition of CSR[15]: While stressing the voluntary nature of CSR, the E.U. commission has been pushing a strong regulatory agenda, without developing any genuine holistic approach to social responsibility.

This leads us to adopt a very ambivalent view of stakeholder theory. While acknowledging the fact that it did effectively provide a major breakthrough by providing businesses with another model, we remain quite skeptical as to its applicability and efficiency in day-to-day operations. Hence the title of this chapter: Stakeholder theory is indeed a challenge since firms must take into account the demands and interests of various stakeholders, though the way of doing so remains extremely *challenging.*

Moving one step further, we will examine in the following section how businesses today actually implement stakeholder management: From talking about stakeholders to eventually walking the talk and integrating stakeholders into both their strategic and day-to-day decisions in order to become more responsible and sustainable.

2. Walking the talk?

Stressing the importance of stakeholders has become commonplace in the business world today. Multinationals as well as the companies reporting on their CSR around the world dedicate the space of one to several pages of their CSR reports to listing their stakeholders, showing that they "proactively listen" to them.

"Stakeholder inclusiveness" as it is now known, is indeed a cornerstone of CSR reporting. It is even the first of the key reporting principles in the opinion of the *Global Reporting Initiative* (GRI).[16] As the organization puts it, the aim is the following:

"The organization should identify its stakeholders, and explain how it has responded to their reasonable expectations and interests.

---

[15] See previous chapter.
[16] See Chapter 1.

> *Stakeholders can include those who are invested in the organization as well as those who have other relationships to the organization. The reasonable expectations and interests of stakeholders are a key reference point for many decisions in the preparation of the report.*"[17]

We can observe that the focus is on the need for the company to show how identifying and providing responses to "reasonable" expectations and interests will help it in the "preparation of the report". That seems to imply that the stakeholder issue is above all a structural basis for reporting. The impact on corporate strategies and operations is not mentioned, which is of course one the main limits of CSR reporting. But more on that later.

The GRI then proposes four stakeholder-related indicators (G4 24 to 27). The first one requires the listing of stakeholders, the second one the process by which the company identified and selected its stakeholders. The next two indicators relate to the responses provided by the companies to their stakeholders, the first one focusing on the approach taken, the *"frequency of engagement"*, whereas the second one requires that the company indicate the *"key topics and concerns that have been raised"* and how the company *"responded"* to them.

As we can see, stakeholder inclusiveness is a two-step process: First a static identification and selection process, then a proactive engagement of the company towards its stakeholders, meaning how the company listened to its stakeholders and what responses it was able to provide.

This formalization process is no doubt useful and positive in the sense that it has compelled companies to consider their stakeholders and start engaging proactively with them. It definitely has had a positive impact regarding the necessary change in mindset.

Indeed, this process prompts companies wishing to report on their CSR to engage in a stakeholder inclusiveness process (whether they are following the GRI guidelines or not). They now "do the job" of identifying their stakeholders and communicating on how they are taking their demands into account. As a result, many current CSR reports include

---

[17] *G4 Guidelines*, GRI, p. 9–10.

smart and colorful diagrams and charts, as well as stakeholder review processes of all kinds…

Once more, the "market of virtue"[18] is playing its part, with consultants coming to the rescue to help companies design their stakeholder approach… "Stakeholder mapping" has become a buzzword among multinationals, which are already familiar with it since it was inspired by a well-established management practice, used for risk assessment for instance. Yet, only a minority of companies have started mapping their stakeholders, as most businesses still concentrate most of their efforts on listing their stakeholders and claiming how much they listen to them…

2.1. *Materiality*

The latest trend in the field of stakeholder management is undoubtedly the materiality review process. Indeed, more and more multinationals have been developing so-called "materiality matrixes" which they usually make publicly available in their CSR reports. These matrixes enable companies to prioritize their CSR actions by confronting stakeholders' expectations

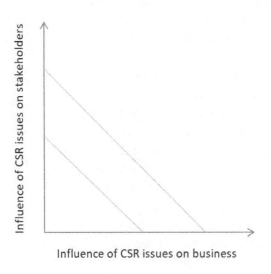

Figure 8:   Simplified materiality matrix

---

[18] See Chapter 1.

with their own business interests and priorities. Materiality must be understood as the business relevance and significance of CSR issues. If supported by a rigorous methodology, this mapping tool can be instrumental in helping the company determine which CSR issues need to be embedded in its strategic vision and plan.

The obvious limit to the applicability of stakeholder matrixes is the methodology used. Indeed, the company first needs to list its key CSR issues, and then prioritize them. But who is in charge of doing this? Ideally the task ought to be performed by a working group representing the key functions of the company including of course CEO and/or top management. Equally critical is the assessment and prioritization of stakeholder expectations: on what basis is this carried out? Which stakeholders are taken into account? How can we weigh their respective importance? According to which data will this analysis be conducted? Once again, a rigorous quantitative and qualitative analysis ideally ought to be carried out based on substantial information (surveys, interviews, panel discussions, etc.) and a well-designed methodology to compound it.

From our own observations and experience, very few companies so far have engaged in a thorough and rigorous process to establish their materiality matrixes. Today, most of them rely on their CSR department to draw up these matrixes based on the information available and with no actual support or input from the rest of the company. Unfortunately, it seems that for the moment these innovative tools are merely seen as external communication gimmicks.

Even when companies engage in a thorough process on materiality (which is the case for many European companies, especially in utilities or agribusiness), the link with the overall strategy remains unclear. Nestlé is a case in point: the Swiss multinational has indeed been working with a team of consultants on its materiality review. The whole process which is publicly available on the Web is quite impressive. Yet at the end of the day, one may wonder what direct impact this has actually had on the company's CSR embeddedness strategy. Perhaps the recent decision by Nestlé to sell off most of its sugar confectionery brands in the U.S.[19] and also New Zealand and Australia is a sign that materiality has

---

[19] Sold to Italian company Ferrero for $2.6 bn.

played a part. Indeed, the top priority that appears in the upper right quadrant of the matrix was "over and under-nutrition"... But apart from that, Nestlé does not seem to have radically revolutionized its way of operating and several social and environmental issues remain highly critical for the firm.

In short, materiality has become a key to the embeddedness process of CSR and in this sense can be viewed as a very positive evolution. Nevertheless, it is more often than not still perceived as nothing more than a communication tool... Not to mention a public relations exercise! The more businesses consider the materiality review as a key management tool and instrument in their strategic vision, the less risk of greenwashing there will be...

2.2. Engaging with stakeholders?

Although companies worldwide are *talking* more and more about their stakeholders in their CSR reports, the key question remains that of the concrete actions taken by companies to engage with their stakeholders and take into account the latter's interests and demands.

Our first observation is that in their reporting on CSR and stakeholders most companies give very little information about what they do in concrete terms. They tend to remain vague, mentioning a few meetings, conferences, events, such as one day during the year when they invite their stakeholders to visit the site.

Some companies do venture further, that is to say by establishing actual consultations that take place once or twice a year, most of the time with local communities and neighborhood groups. This is especially the case for extractive and manufacturing industries that have a harmful impact on their local environment. These consultations often take the form of panel discussions. Pictures are displayed, videos are uploaded, but very little is said about the outcome of such consultations. The focus is usually on dialogue rather than actual decisions taken as a result.

In this respect, a growing practice is that of stakeholder panels who are supposed to be representative of the company's key stakeholders on CSR. One of the pioneers in this area was French cement multinational Lafarge; as early as 2003, it set up a ten-member panel of external stakeholders representing civil society and experts on social and environmental issues. The panel used to meet twice a year and issue an uncensored, collective, statement on Lafarge's CSR policy. Several panel members testified to the fact that they were not paid and remained fully independent in their discernment and assessment work.[20] Even though the French company merged with Swiss multinational Holcim, the panel has remained active, although it has been renamed the *External Report Review Panel* and is comprised of only six members. Its review can be found in the company's latest CSR report: In a two-page document, the panel clearly points out both positive aspects[21] and areas for improvement.

All in all, very few companies actually describe which actions involving all of their main stakeholders they undertake. As we will see below, priority is usually given to some specific stakeholders such as NGOs or suppliers. CSR actions with customers or employees are rarely mentioned. They appear to be confined to their original spheres, i.e. marketing for the former and human resources management for the latter.

Among good practices identified around the world, a strikingly comprehensive effort can be found in the latest CSR report issued by Lebanon's leading bank Bank Audi. Indeed, the bank chose to select ten stakeholders, employees, management, shareholders, suppliers, clients, regulatory bodies and industry-related associations, NGOs, competitors, community/civil society and media. A comprehensible table was then drawn up,[22] comprising for each stakeholder *"the basis of selection, channels used, issues identified in 2016 and implemented in 2017, and issues identified in 2017"*. This table actually provides concrete information on the CSR actions undertaken as a result of consultations with the respective stakeholders. In addition, the bank bases its materiality review on a consistent approach, relying on a comprehensive employee survey of CSR priorities, among other sources.

---

[20] See for instance Alastair McIntosh's testimony. An activist and strong opponent of Lafarge, he finally agreed to join the panel. www.alastairmcintosh.com/general/quarry/lafarge-panel.htm, retrieved on August 16, 2018.

[21] Considering for instance the company's response to the highly critical Syrian affair (see Chapter 1) as quite transparent.

[22] See CSR Report 2017, *Committed*, Bank Audi, pp. 53–57.

The main difficulty today clearly lies in the fact that there is very limited implementation of stakeholder consultation among businesses: Apart from a handful of actively engaged companies, stakeholder management remains a nice theoretical framework with very little concrete impact on strategic and operational decision-making processes.

An innovative initiative I had the chance to take part in was the elaboration of "guiding principles for a constructive dialogue with stakeholders" in 2016.[23] Initiated by Comité 21, a French "do tank" organization dedicated to implementing sustainability in the wake of the 1992 Rio summit, the final document was the result of a multi-stakeholder collaboration process which eventually led to the adoption of an in-depth and practical methodological guide based on seven overarching principles:

1) Have the willingness and the means to change.
2) Take into account diverse, even diverging interests.
3) Commit to choosing relevant stakeholders and issues.
4) Involve all stakeholders by appointing an internal or external facilitator.
5) Respect dialogue values.
6) Anchor the process in the long-term.
7) Report the results to all actors.

The objective was to provide companies with a voluntary and practical methodology to concretely enter into a constructive dialogue with several stakeholders who impact the governance and strategy. The principles and the guide were officially published and endorsed by the French Ministry for the Environment, and have so far been signed by over 25 leading French companies. A key contribution was to provide a clear step-by-step methdology for businesses and to stress the need for a facilitator.

---

[23] *Principes directeurs pour un dialogue constructif avec les parties prenantes,* co-constructed by Comité 21 and multiple stakeholders (companies, NGOs, labor unions, local government, trade federations, independent experts, academics). Retrieved from www.comite21.org/docs/dialogue-pp/principes-directeurs-pour-un-dialogue-constructif-avec-les-parties-prenantes.pdf

In summary, while several innovative initiatives on consultations and dialogue with stakeholders can be observed, the tangible impacts of such attempts remain very limited. In the case of most businesses, the stakeholder issue is an attractive concept from the CSR department standpoint. However, this does not really impact the company as a whole in its strategy and operations. At the end of the day, only bilateral collaborations with selected stakeholders tend to lead to concrete actions being taken. Let us now examine these new forms of partnering, with a focus on NGOs since they are unique stakeholders when it comes to the CSR agenda.

2.3. Partnering with stakeholders?

NGOs are indeed very special stakeholders since their *raison d'être* is intrinsically linked to the CSR agenda. As non-for-profit independent civil society organizations, they stand out as privileged partners. It goes without saying that such stakeholders as employees, suppliers or government are critical categories of stakeholders, but we shall deal with them later on when tackling more specific aspects of the CSR agenda.

Partnerships with NGOs have been in vogue since the late 1990s, which corresponds to the rise of NGOs on the international CSR scene. In addition, the U.N. 2002 Johannesburg Summit saw the highest number of international NGOs take part and engage in so-called type II partnerships[24] with several multinationals. Since then, hundreds of companies worldwide have developed CSR programs with NGOs.

Nevertheless, most of these "partnerships" are of the philanthropic type: NGOs in this case are entrusted with the funds donated by a company for a charitable cause. These programs are quite developed in the U.S. of course, but also in the developing world where NGOs are quite numerous. According to James E. Austin,[25] the philanthropic type is the minimal type of company-NGO partnership: Indeed, the NGOs in this case are mere instruments and no one really cares about how efficient how efficiently the money allocated is used. What counts is the fact that the

---

[24] Type II partnerships are partnerships which do not involve public actors.
[25] See Austin, J. (2001). "Strategic Collaboration Between Nonprofits and Business". *Nonprofit and Voluntary Sector Quarterly* 29(1), 69–97.

company donated money to "do good". One of the consequences of this widespread practice is the poor reputation of NGOs in many parts of the world, since many of them are poorly managed and more often than not corrupt. In the developing world, it is indeed a fact that most NGOs are connected to the government, to communities with vested interests or to wealthy individuals.

The second type identified by Austin is the "transactional type". In this type, there is a reciprocal interest for both parties to engage in a partnership, i.e. money, resources for the NGO, image and local access and knowledge for the company. Many of these transactional partnerships which developed in the 2000s are promoted by companies as CSR programs helping them to achieve their CSR objectives. The typical types of such partnerships are sponsorship and co-branding strategies whereby NGOs "lend" their image and their logo, thus helping companies develop more environmentally or socially conscious products. From fair trade or fair labor labels to co-branded credit cards, examples abound around the world.

But upon closer examination, it appears that there is a discrepancy between the way the partnership is promoted and the concrete achievements on the ground. Yet, these partnerships help companies move towards compliance-based CSR; they also bring together two very different worlds, enabling both sides to learn more about each other.

The third category and the most promising one in our eyes is what Austin defines as the "integrative" type of partnership. In these cases both parties agree on a multi-annual agenda, engaging in a long-term joint project in which both the company and the NGO stand on equal footing. Missions, people and activities tend to merge. Crucial to the implementation of such ambitious agreements are the ability on both sides to develop constructive dialogue eventually leading to a common language.[26]

Among these types of partnerships, let us cite the pioneering case of French cement company Lafarge which in 2000 signed their first five-year agreement with World Wildlife Fund (WWF) International focusing on climate change and biodiversity. The partnership was renewed in

---

[26] See for instance Selsky & Parker, 2005; Jonker & Nijhol, 2006; and Jamali & Keshishian, 2009.

2005 and again in 2009, with a broader agenda and strengthened cooperation. As Lafarge said, the WWF was a "critical" friend. It is true that
this long-term partnership was far from easy to sustain: Several crises
occurred between the two parties, some of which had a critical impact
on Lafarge's activity.[27] Then, while many saw mostly greenwashing in
the agreement (denouncing the rather "soft" position of the NGO regarding the business world), others pointed out its effective achievements.
Whatever the limits of the program may have been, substantial results
were obtained, especially regarding biodiversity and quarry rehabilita-
tion. Indeed, Lafarge soon became known as a pioneer in the industry
since it had committed to rehabilitating most of its quarries. This gave
the company a competitive advantage in many parts of the world where
the local stakeholders, including local government, were pleased with
the company's engagements.[28] Without WWF's expertise, this could
never have happened. Technical expertise is probably one of the most
tangible contributions provided by NGOs.

More recently, in the social field, the partnership initiated in 2013
between British pharmaceutical giant GlaxoSmithKline (GSK) and the
NGO Save the Children is undoubtedly another interesting example. The
five-year partnership, operating in Kenya and the Congo, aimed to save
the lives of one million children by the year 2018. Two years later, the
results were quite impressive since 300,000 children had been saved. To
do that, three million pounds were raised, enabling GSK's expertise to be
transferred to the ground, with Save the Children providing knowledge
about the local environment. Both parties have claimed that they truly
learned from each other and, in addition to an improved brand image for
GSK, the numbers are quite impressive and this partnership has helped the
company find some adequate responses to children's mortality in poor
environments, which definitely represents a medium-term strategic advantage for it.

---

[27] As Lafarge in 2009 was about to exploit a sand deposit on the French Atlantic coast next
to a European protected area, the WWF threatened to withdraw from the agreement. As a
result, Lafarge gave up the project.
[28] Abandoned quarries are known to cause severe and lasting damage to the environment
(soil erosion, water depletion, etc.).

Today though, such partnerships remain quite exceptional. Even more strikingly, there has not been much literature on the subject since the late 2000s. One of the reasons may be that there have been many failures among the existing partnerships. Moreover, there is constant skepticism about company-NGO partnerships given the inherent obstacles. Indeed, finding the right convergence between market-driven and common interest logics is no easy task. In addition, the risks are high for both parties: For the companies, accusations of green- or social washing are common, and shareholders are usually quite suspicious about such deals. With regard to NGOs, credibility and legitimacy are at risk, all the more so as the issue of NGO financial dependence is widely criticized. On top of that, NGOs risk losing the confidence of their members, which could eventually jeopardize the future of the organization itself.

Yet, we do believe that strategic partnerships between companies and NGOs will contribute to strategic CSR implementation. The solution may reside in the current evolution of corporate foundations which are gradually moving away from traditional philanthropy to engage in longer term strategic approaches. This is especially the case in Europe today.

The other positive role endorsed by NGOs today is that of change makers in several industries: Indeed, international NGOs specialized in designing new industry labels also act as monitoring agencies, helping businesses adopt new codes of conduct and new supply chain practices. Two such cases are the Fair Labor Association for labor practices, and Max Havelaar or Rainforest Alliance for suppliers' relations. Major environmental NGOs such as the WWF or Greenpeace (which has also started to collaborate with business) are also involved in developing new industry standards,[29] thus contributing to more sustainable practices.

2.4. A challenge for ever?

In spite of all the trendy rhetoric around stakeholders, one must recognize that an overwhelming majority of businesses haven't found how to take

---

[29] Among these standards, one can cite FSC for forestry, MSC for fisheries or RSPO for palm oil.

their key stakeholders' expectations about CSR into account in a genuine and consistent way. The challenge remains, and the stakes are high.

Yet, some innovative practices have emerged in the last few years: Several multinationals are attempting to measure the value they create for their key stakeholders. This is taking place mostly within the context of integrated reporting approaches.[30] Even though the methodology and the results remain uncertain, this is a positive evolution to the extent that it aims at linking stakeholders to performance.

But at the end of the day, this has little impact on the overall performance approach of companies. As long as companies are driven by stockholders' maximization demands, stakeholder management will largely remain a P.R. issue, and at best in very few cases an innovative attempt to break down value creation.

The crux of the matter is clearly to be found in the law. A company/corporation is by law acting in the interest of its owners, i.e. the stockholders who are expecting the best return on their investments. Only legal changes are likely to bring about a new equilibrium between the expectations of stockholders and those of other key stakeholders.

In other words, it is high time corporate charters around the world included social and environmental considerations so that profit-driven goals do not remain the sole objective. Positive changes are taking place around the world, notably in the Anglo-Saxon countries. The Benefit Corporation (B-Corp) status we have already looked at is one; we can also mention the community interest company status created in the United Kingdom in 2005. More than 10,000 organizations have opted for this status since it was created. In the U.S. several states have set up social purpose corporations; the same movement is happening in Canada and Australia. France is considering changing its corporate law to make it obligatory for companies to take into account the social and environmental consequences of their actions.

These examples demonstrate that a new trend is emerging and is likely to have a profound impact on corporate strategies and activities in the years to come. And this would obviously bring the stakeholders to the fore. In other words, walking the talk on stakeholders may eventually become true.

---

[30]The issue of integrated reporting is tackled in Chapter 6.

CHAPTER 3

THE "BLIND SPOT" OF CSR? SOCIAL DIALOGUE AND POLICIES

Everybody would agree on the fact that employees are key stakeholders of CSR. Employee support and involvement seems empirically fundamental to the deployment of CSR policies within the company. This intuition was already present at the birth of the CSR concept: Indeed, one of Bowen's main preoccupations in his seminal book was that of adequate labor supply. He firmly believed that a socially responsible company would both attract the best talent and enhance employee morale.

Since then, it has more or less been taken for granted that employees were at the core of CSR. Yet, the theoretical debate over CSR seems to have focused much more on external issues such as the environment, the supply chain or local communities than on internal social issues. Some even go as far as stating that the *social*, i.e. human resource dimension of CSR, has been largely ignored.[1] Suffice to say that the amount of literature on CSR-related internal social issues is rather scarce; the same goes for the necessary convergence between human resource management and CSR which is crucial but rarely discussed.

This chapter intends to examine a striking illustration of this gap, namely that of workers' representation and its relation to CSR. As previously mentioned, workers' representatives, labor unions, have hardly

---

[1]French expert Jacques Igalens talked of "the social dimension as the *unthought of* CSR" ("*le social comme impensé de la RSE*").

77

ever been considered as stakeholders of CSR. Apart from a few neo-institutional academics[2] in continental Europe, workers' unions are not mentioned at all in Anglo-Saxon literature. This of course may be due to the fact that unionization has dropped considerably in the U.S. and Great Britain. Yet, unions are still present in many companies in these countries. Furthermore, unionization is a universal reality, from continental Europe to the developing world. Besides, it is one of the core ILO Conventions, *Convention 6 on Freedom of Association and Collective Bargaining*. Even though unions may take very different forms around the world, the fact that they have been "expelled" from the CSR debate remains a mystery.

Even in continental Europe where "social dialogue" is the cornerstone of industrial relations, workers' unions seem to remain remote from the CSR arena. Rather than stakeholders of CSR, they appear as "stakeseekers".[3] Why is that so? Why are they not fully involved in CSR whereas many CSR issues such as health and wellbeing at work are clearly connected to their agenda? We shall attempt first to analyze the reasons why social dialogue is by and large a "blind spot" of CSR.

In a recent study[4] conducted by European-based non-financial rating agency Vigéo Eiris, it appeared that no more than 4% of companies world-wide issued a formalized commitment (based on public documents) to conduct social dialogue with employee representatives. Conversely, 62% of companies made no commitment on social dialogue, even though they communicated objectives and indicators on the quality of their relation-ships with customers and shareholders, or regarding environmental protection.

As anticipated, companies based in Europe performed better than their peers on social dialogue, with an average score of 38/100, compared to 17/100 for North American companies, 19/100 for Asia Pacific companies

---

[2] See for instance Preuss, 2008, 2009; and Delbard, 2011.

[3] Holzer, B.: "Turning Stakeseekers Into Stakeholders", *Business and Society*, 47(1), pp. 50–67, 2008.

[4] "Social Dialogue: A Social Corporate Responsibility 'Blind Spot'", 2018. Retrieved from http://www.vigeo-eiris.com/wp-content/uploads/2018/06/20180612_SF_Dialogue-Social-.pdf

and 26/100 for Emerging Market companies. Yet, only 11% of companies in Europe addressed CSR issues in their collective bargaining.

Why is this so? As already pointed out, employees are by nature core stakeholders of CSR, and social dialogue is strongly institutionalized in Europe. Does this mean that the institutional European context has made CSR so implicit[5] that it does not connect with the social agenda? I often refer to a telling anecdote: As I was conducting a research project in Germany, several respondents insisted that "CSR does not exist in Germany". Social regulation was so extensive that the mere idea of voluntary social issues being discussed between management and their employees did not make any sense to them. Social dialogue was supposed to lead to full-fledged regulations. Yet, a strong convergence between social dialogue and CSR would undoubtedly bridge a gap.

1. CSR and social dialogue at the national level in Europe

A research I conducted in 2011 and based on three European countries (France, Germany and Great Britain) showed very few connections between social dialogue and CSR. Strikingly enough, most trade unions representatives interviewed appeared suspicious of CSR and reluctant to endorse CSR issues such as human rights, well-being at work or subcontracting. For British and German unions, CSR issues were new and external to the traditional social agenda. French unions disagreed with each other; as some were viewing CSR as a natural extension of the social agenda, others considered it as an inconsistent concept and managerial "trap" meant to deprive unions of their institutional role and influence.[6]

Several factors clearly account for these positions. First, trade unionism has considerably lost of its influence over the last decades, as an aftermath of globalization and the emergence of global supply chains. Furthermore, the decline of blue collar jobs has brought about the decline, even maybe the end of a collective work logic. In parallel, social rights

---

[5] See Matten & Moon, Chapter 1.

[6] Delbard, O.: "Social Partners of Full-Fledged Stakeholders? Trade Unions and CSR in Europe", *Society and Business Review*, 6, pp. 260–277, 2011.

have been gradually privatized through unilateral codes of ethics.[7] At the same time, the rise of sustainability-related issues has been pushing companies to turn to other stakeholders such as NGOs — providing hardly any connection with unions.

Faced with these disruptive changes, trade unions urgently need to redefine their roles and positions. It is high time they shifted from "*a culture of representation to a culture of commitment*" as a French historian put it.[8]

This way, unions could turn into "*in-house NGOs*"[9] and eventually become full-fledged stakeholders.[10] Unions are perfectly legitimate when it comes to the social agenda. An extended agenda including CSR-related issues would be a real opportunity for them to extend their influence and look into the future. But cultural obstacles still abound, due to national work cultures and representations. Once more, CSR is often viewed as a liberal anti-union trick performed by management.

Our findings led us to assert that the European level might well be more appropriate, since both the concepts of transnational social dialogue and CSR have been officially endorsed by the European Union.

2. CSR and social dialogue within the European Union

The French and German schools of CSR assert that social dialogue at the European level is indeed the "normative core" of socially-related CSR,[11] meaning that all CSR policies should derive from the institutional reality. In addition, given the remaining differences among E.U. countries in terms of social legislations, the transnational level seems the most adequate to handle the CSR agenda. In reality, transational social dialogue has officially emerged at the E.U. level within the last two decades, with

---

[7] Preuss, L.: "A Reluctant Stakeholder? On the Perception of Corporate Social Responsibility Among European Trade Unions", *Business Ethics: A European Review*, 17, 2008.

[8] Rosanvallon, P.: "*Democratic Universalism as a Historical Problem*", doi.org, 2009.

[9] Preuss, 2008.

[10] Delbard, 2011.

[11] Lépineux in Bonnafoux-Boucher & Pesqueux, 2006.

the establishment in 1994[12] of European works councils for companies with more than 1,000 employees in the E.U. and at least more than 150 in at least two countries.

These transnational negotiation fora can certainly be the right place for an extended social dialogue encompassing CSR issues. Besides, the representative body for trade unions at the European level, the ETUC,[13] has added some CSR issues, mostly environmental, to its traditional social agenda. Yet, it is also well known that traditional union culture tends to reject environmentalism, seeing it as antagonistic to the defense of social rights. This view, though considered to be obsolete by some "progressive"[14] unions, is still pervasive among unionists. This is all the more detrimental to the future of unionism as unions were actively involved in the 2011 European revised definition of CSR, whereas they had not participated in the 2001 definition process.

At the end of the day, trade unions remain cautious about CSR. Whereas they tend to acknowledge the importance of environment and climate-related issues, they remain engrossed on the traditional social agenda. This is rather unfortunate since many CSR-related issues are quite important today and not necessarily covered by legislation. These finally remain within the scope of NGO activism. In addition, research has shown very few connections between trade unions and NGOs in Europe. The case of the Anglo-Saxon world is even more striking since NGOs have definitely won over trade unions. In turn, the remaining unions tend to behave as NGOs.[15]

3. CSR and social dialogue at the global scale: The case for International Framework Agreements?

With the advent of globalization, multinational companies started to negotiate agreements with international union federations representing national unions in given industries. Whereas the first so-called

---

[12] The Directive on employee representation was revised in 2009.
[13] European Trade Union Confederation.
[14] Such as the French Democratic Confederation of Labor (CFDT).
[15] This is especially the case in Great Britain with the TUC (Trade Union Congress).

International or Global Framework Agreements were signed in the late 1980s, the number of such agreements multiplied between 2000 and 2008.

These agreements usually list key social issues to be agreed upon between the multinational companies and the international unions representing affiliated local unions. Even though these bilateral agreements are non-binding, they have been recognized by the ILO since they embody the willingness to lay down rules and guidelines at a transnational level. For some, they are typically hybrid instruments, situated halfway between soft law and hard law.[16] Seen from another angle, they appear to be a typical example of private social regulation instruments.

Up until very recently, International Framework Agreements were mostly examined by lawyers keen to stress the limited impacts of such engagements on dispute resolutions. From a CSR perspective, some researchers started to investigate the contents of such agreements, since CSR-related issues were expected to be found. In addition, new stakeholders of CSR were emerging at the global level, namely these little known international union federations.

The results were quite disappointing: Even though many agreements did include some CSR clauses such as supply chain-, health- or environment-related issues, the monitoring of these agreements appeared to be quite shaky. Some research showed that one of the few benefits was to establish direct contacts between top management at the Head Office and international Federation leaders, making it easier to resolve local social conflicts occurring within subsidiaries.[17]

Today, even though a second generation of Global Framework Agreements has emerged with seemingly more efficient dispute-resolution procedures as well as a wider range of CSR-related issues, these instruments remain a *blind spot* of CSR. This is sadly confirmed by the fact that Global Framework Agreements do not appear in the ISO 26000 framework. Whereas these agreements seem to favor unionization at the local level, the link with CSR does not appear.

---

[16] Sobczak, A.: "Ensuring the effective implementation of transnational company agreements", *European Journal of Industrial Relations*, 18(2), pp. 139–151 (2012).
[17] Delbard, 2012.

As a survey pointed out, these agreements are merely reflections of the CSR approaches taken by multinational companies:

"While all TNCs with IFAs have some kind of policy on corporate social responsibility and regard their IFA as an additional element of that, the efforts expended by management to ensure the implementation of the IFA depend significantly on the extent to which management has endorsed corporate social responsibility as an integral element of all its business operations. In light of the fact that the vast majority of IFAs have been negotiated with TNCs with headquarters in the E.U., the legal and institutional environment also seems to have had a significant impact". [18]

In other words, multinational companies with embedded CSR strategies are more likely to have signed such agreements, especially if they are European. This is evidenced by the fact that the majority of Global Framework Agreements have indeed been signed with European companies.

The same trend was evidenced by the much mediatized and dramatic case of the Rana Plaza building collapse in 2013.

4. Lessons from the Rana Plaza case

In 2013, the collapse of an eight-story building took place in a suburban area of Dhaka, the capital of Bangladesh. This resulted in the deaths of over 1,100 people and more than 2,500 injured survivors. These victims were garment workers, mostly women and children, employed by the subcontractors of well-known international fashion brands, such as Benetton and Primark. One of the poorest countries in the world, Bangladesh heavily relies on the textile industry, which accounts for 80% of its exports.

The day before the collapse, some cracks had been discovered within the building. Consequently, safety inspectors had immediately called for

---

[18] Fichter, M., Helfen, M., & Sydow, J.: "Regulating Labor Relations in Global Production Networks: Insights on International Framework Agreements". *Internationale Politik und Gesellschaft*, 2(2011), pp. 69–86, 2011.

the closure of the building. Whereas bank employees and other apartment dwellers did leave the premises, the garment workers who had expressed their worries to their employers were forced to report for work on the following day. At 9 am, right after the beginning of work, the fatal collapse happened, as had been predicted.

This tragedy led to an unprecedented binding agreement between multinational companies and international and local labor unions. Launched in May 2013, the *Fire and Building Safety Accord* was the first of its kind: A transnational private governance agreement was indeed signed for a period of five years with the aim to inspect and improve the working conditions at more than 2,000 garment factories in the country. Within a few months, over 200 garment multinationals signed it along with two global unions, UNI Global Union and IndustriALL, and a Bangladeshi union named The United Federation of Garment Workers. Some NGOs among which the Clean Clothes Campaign and the Workers Rights Consortium were granted observer status. The Accord was chaired by a neutral party, the UN's International Labor Office (ILO).

For the first time in history, Western multinationals were engaging in a multi-annual financial and legal agreement aiming to improve the working conditions of subcontracted employees. Within five years, the fund did reach the targeted 30 million dollars. Over 1,600 factories were inspected, a few were closed down and according to the official statistics, 80% of the inspections led to remediation measures.

What is striking is that most of the Accord's signatories were European (out of the 200 signatories, less than twenty were North-American). In parallel to the Accord, North American multinationals set up the Alliance, whereby they committed to engaging in discussions with local worker representatives with a view to improving safety and working conditions. Nevertheless, all studies agree on the fact that even though both the Accord and the Alliance had the same goals, the Alliance was definitely less binding than the Accord, with no official direct representation of workers' unions and no liability risks for the multinationals involved.

The creation of these two unique agreements does provide groundbreaking insights into the evolution of CSR practices in the context of global supply chains. First, it shows how important the issue of subcontracted supply chains has become for companies. Conscious of the inherent reputational risk, multinationals cannot afford to ignore the issues at stake and rely solely on suppliers' codes of conduct and social audits. Pushed by their CSR departments, they have to offer concrete assistance and solutions to local workers, even though the latter are not directly employed by them. The globalization momentum of trade and CSR issues had definitely had a major impact on supply chain management practices since the first historic case of Nike in the mid-1990s.[19]

Furthermore, the split between a European approach and a North American one clearly exemplifies the existence of two main types of CSR approaches around the world as was already explained above: The European approach is more implicit since it is far more embedded in the institutional regulatory context, whereas the North American approach remains more explicit, i.e. mostly engineered by the business world itself. What the two approaches have in common though is the growing realization that a proactive CSR approach is urgently needed to respond to the reputational risks related to global supply chains.

This also illustrates what was mentioned earlier in this chapter, namely the fact that social dialogue is embedded in European practices: The Accord clearly demonstrates it. By negotiating directly with international and local unions, the Accord signatories showed their readiness to push what was originally a CSR issue towards binding engagements and rules.

Surprisingly enough, the Accord, which was terminated in July 2018, was renewed for a transition period of 3 years, the ultimate goal being to transfer the responsibility of improving safety and working conditions to the Government of Bangladesh by 2021. Whereas most of the first Accord signatories have renewed their engagements, what is most interesting to examine are the new priorities stressed by the agreement. Indeed, the

---

[19] Nike had completely outsourced its production, and thus was accused of ignoring the fact that its products were all too often produced in horrible conditions by pregnant women or children in third world Asian countries. Faced with public opinion uproar, the U.S. company responded by hiring social inspectors to perform audits among the subcontractors. Because of the scandal, Nike's sales sagged and the stock price fell dramatically for a while.

focus is clearly on workers' rights: Those of joining unions, the ease of filing complaints and receiving fair compensation.

Indeed, all the independent studies carried out on the 2013 agreement showed mixed results. While inspections were indeed carried out leading to some significant improvements, many striking problems remained unanswered. Access to unionization remained extremely limited, factory closures led to massive job dismissals with no severance payments for most workers,[20] inspections were limited and recommendations not always applicable to the local context.[21]

The most striking weakness of the Accord is undoubtedly its very limited impact on workers' access to representation through unions. Today in Bangladesh, no more than 200,000 workers in 445 factories are represented by unions. Moreover, a survey conducted by the Bangladesh Garment Worker Unity Forum in 2015 found that 98% of garment workers had never heard of either the Accord or Alliance.[22]

This lack of knowledge can largely be linked to the narrow breadth of local unions and global federations involved. The signatories of the Accord were indeed a well-connected, English-speaking minority. In addition, access to unionization has been made difficult by all the legal and practical barriers put in place by the Bangladeshi government.[23] On top of that, it appears that the signatory companies did not make any effort to lift these barriers, as this was not a mandatory requirement of the Accord.

More generally speaking, the Accord excluded many factories not meeting the criteria, such as the myriads of informal or semi-formal small shops functioning as Tier 2 suppliers, i.e. subcontractors for larger factories. They were not subjected to it since they had no direct link with international buyers. A study[24] pointed out *"the routine practice of subcontracting, often through purchasing agents, and in a manner that is not transparent to*

---

[20] In 2014, 14 garment factories were closed, leading to 14,000 job losses. Most of the workers did not get any compensation even though the Accord had included a clause about it.

[21] Labowitz & Baumann-Pauly: *Business as usual is not an option*, Center for Business and Human Rights, 2014.

[22] Tanjeem, N.: "Thinking beyond Accord and alliance", *The Daily Star*, published May 22, 2017.

[23] *Ibid.*

[24] Labowitz & Baumann-Pauly, 2014.

buyers or regulators" and where brutal worker exploitation prevails. Not to mention leather tanneries or factories producing household textiles where workers are even more vulnerable.

In short, private regulation engineered by companies, international organisations and NGOs may help improve the working conditions of tier one suppliers, but only a systematic approach involving the brands, unions, primary suppliers and the government can help meet minimum standards in all the country's factories. The new Accord signed in 2018 rightly stressed the need to support workers in being represented and defended.

On the positive side, the Accord has had some tangible impact on the Bangladeshi government: After having slightly increased the minimum wage in the garment industry shortly after the Rana Plaza collapse, the government announced a 51% increase in September 2018, to 95 U.S. dollars a month. Yet, unions rightly claim that this is far from sufficient as the cost of living in Dhaka is as high as in some Western capitals.

As for the Alliance, the results look even more questionable, with very few tangible results. All in all, it looks much more like a classic CSR program where companies alone have the lead. This the reason why I believe the Accord to be really innovative, despite all the flaws listed above.

To conclude, it seems that several lessons may be drawn from the Rana Plaza case:

— Involving trade unions fully is the only way of pushing the CSR agenda further when it comes to global supply chains. This means finding the right balance between CSR policies with their soft law approach and local regulation. In other words, labor issues triggered by CSR inevitably raise the question of the need for hard law.

— The results met locally will never be fully achieved without mounting CSR awareness at the local level. This means that multinationals have a key responsibility in helping local subcontractors integrate CSR into their operations. But this requires that multinationals no longer send paradoxical injunctions to their suppliers. To put it bluntly, how can local manufacturers embed CSR principles if their clients keep asking for very short delivery deadlines which inevitably mean overtime for workers or turning to informal local subcontracting!

— This in turn requires that multinational companies further embed CSR into their strategic vision, which implies profound changes in marketing strategies and supply chain operations. The Rana Plaza case does show the link between CSR, marketing and supply chain. Indeed, signing the Accord does have direct repercussions on the supply chain and marketing strategies.

— Which in the end, supposes that it is up to us consumers to start changing our consumption habits. Regarding fashion, a revolution is needed, based on a "less is more" approach. Fast fashion is definitely not sustainable…

5. A priority for the CSR agenda of tomorrow?

This chapter demonstrates that employee-related issues are a blind spot of CSR today. Indeed, whereas they seem crucial to us, they seem to be hanging in a no man's land between the well-established community-based view of CSR (mostly through philanthropy) and the more recent environment-related approach (through sustainability).

One of the reasons might well be that social policies pertain to Human Resource Management (HRM) and that the line between social policies and CSR actions is unclear. The very limited amount of literature on the interactions between HRM and CSR somewhat testifies to it.

When it comes to social dialogue and worker representation from a geographical perspective, three main concerns need to be considered:

1) The U.S. and its zone of influence where the question has been largely ignored since CSR theory from the start failed to recognize workers' unions as stakeholders of CSR.

2) Continental Europe, where social dialogue is the cornerstone of labor relations and CSR implicitly embedded in the institutional settings.

3) The developing world, where on the contrary social dialogue and employee-related issues appear to be top priorities on the CSR agenda as the Rana Plaza case showed it.[25]

---

[25] See Chapter 5.

This focus on employees and their representation leads me to highlight two key issues regarding the future of CSR: First, the global diffusion of CSR through global value chains clearly brings the internal social issues to the fore, or to put it differently, is likely to generate a third approach to CSR in which company-related social issues play a vital role, along with local government involvement. This question will be examined further in the next chapter on human rights and CSR.

CHAPTER 4

HUMAN RIGHTS AND CSR — A LONG WAY TO GO

Whereas the relation between CSR and employee representation seems to remain largely ignored, the question of human rights has become a key issue of the CSR agenda over the last 10 years.

This is definitely an emerging trend in CSR; indeed, up until the 2000s, human rights were mostly viewed as a political issue to be handled by international and national public bodies. If we follow Karel Vasak's typology of human rights,[1] three waves of human rights have been identified throughout history.

The first historic wave emerged in the 18th century in Europe and was based on some fundamental rights to liberty, namely individual and political freedoms. This first wave coincides with the rise of the concept of modern democracy in Western Europe. The second wave was born in the wake of World War II, with the groundbreaking 1948 U.N. Universal Declaration of Human Rights. The focus at that time was on the rights to equality which States were urged to grant. Such rights as the right to education, to health, to social security, to work, to organize and to assemble were then recognized and confirmed by the U.N. Assembly. Compared to the 18th century when human rights were purely an individual matter, the question was from then on intrinsically related to individual States' responsibility.

---

[1] See for instance his book *The International Dimensions of Human Rights* published in 1982.

Finally, in the 1980s appeared a third wave of human rights in relation to the constitution of a new globalized world coupled with the emergence of the sustainable development concept. The third generation of rights is focused on solidarity, with such new rights as environmental rights, the rights of minorities and indigenous peoples, the right to development, peace, democracy, self-determination, etc. The major change with this third generation of rights was the assumption that such rights would be granted thanks to the combined efforts of all, meaning, not only the States, but also the representatives of civil society... And the private sector.

1. From the political realm to the CSR arena

The newly established relation between business and human rights is clearly due to the globalization process and the consequential growing power and influence of multinational companies.

1.1. The consequences of globalization (mid 1980s–2010)

Indeed, globalization has had numerous effects on the organization of labor and the respective powers of political and economic actors. With the opening up of developing country economies appeared global value chains, with Western companies starting to outsource their production facilities to developing countries in the late 1980s and early 1990s. This enabled companies to increase their power by reducing their costs and achieving economies of scale on the one hand and to exert political influence around the world thanks to their presence in multiple markets.

This movement was backed up by the information revolution which enabled instant transfer of data and information around the world. Beyond the well-identified impact this technological revolution has had on capitalism, a major consequence on the CSR agenda was the emergence of a global civil society, better informed and ready to act against the social and environmental evils generated by globalization. International NGOs and watchdog organizations became major players in the new world order.

In the field of human rights, Amnesty International, Human Rights Watch and the International Federation for Human Rights which used to be solely focused on the political aspects of multinational corporations started to look into their behavior, assessing their impacts on human rights. Sector-based watchdog organizations also appeared, such as the Clean Clothes Campaign for the garment industry and the Responsible Sourcing Network;[2] they became prominent voices on highly sensitive issues such as the working conditions of developing country subcontractors.

Yet, up until recently, the questions of human rights were not clearly associated with CSR. In spite of numerous environmental and social disasters caused by multinational corporations in the developing world over the years, the dominant view was that these were political issues to be handled by competent national and/or international authorities. The most symbolic and tragic case was that of the Bhopal Disaster which occurred in 1984 in India and is likely to have directly caused thousands of injuries and at least 18,000 deaths. The disaster was caused by a toxic gas leak in a pesticide plant owned by U.S. company Union Carbide Corporation. After numerous lawsuits initiated by both Indian and U.S. courts, seven former employees were sentenced to two years of imprisonment in 2010 in India. For its part, Union Carbide offered ridiculously low amounts of compensation money for the victims. A first settlement took place in 1986, whereby Union Carbide agreed to pay around USD 400 million. Their subsequent offers were turned down by the Indian government. At the end of the day, this case demonstrated the inability for the parties to reach satisfactory conclusions be it by law or through compensation money.

In the following years and decades, the same unsatisfactory situation continued. In most environmental and social disasters caused by multinationals, litigation proved weak and inoperative; multinationals resorted to financial compensation in the traditional philanthropic sense. Settlements (a.k.a. "hush" money) were usually provided to the local communities affected by the disaster but they were not given any satisfactory long-term solution.

These practices reflect the trend toward corporate citizenship which in its dominant form was nothing more than an updated globalized version

---

[2]The Responsible Sourcing Network is an emanation of the non-profit organization As You Sow, a leader in shareholder advocacy for CSR.

of traditional philanthropy.³ Regarding the sectors of activity most affected, extractive industries were the most exposed at first, followed by the garment and agribusiness industries later on, and more recently by ITC (information and communication technology) companies.

1.2. The case of Total in Myanmar: Towards a managerial approach to human rights

With the increasing momentum of globalization and the acceleration of the information revolution in the 21ˢᵗ century, human rights issues related to corporate activity became more and more acute and mediatized. An emblematic case is that of the French oil and gas multinational Total and its operations in Myanmar.

As a member of a consortium, Total signed a 30-year contract in 1992 to exploit offshore gas in Myanmar. The gas was to be transported to Thailand through a pipeline built by Total and its partners,⁴ and the State-owned Myanmarese company MOGE was to be provided with a substantial share of the profits. Myanmar was known at the time to be one of the worst military dictatorships on the planet. In addition, the project, named Yadana, was located in an area populated by an ethnic minority, the Karen, who were severely oppressed by the central government.

Following the start of the project in 1995 and the first gas delivery in 1998, Total was under pressure from international NGOs, such as EarthRights International which accused the multinational of being an accomplice to major human rights violations such as rape, torture, expulsions and even killings in the pipeline area. One of the main reasons for these accusations was the company's alleged reliance on the national armed forces to ensure the security in the area. Several reports commissioned by international NGOs to assess the situation raised concern about the severe human rights violations related to the Yadana project. However,

---

³ See Chapter 1.
⁴ The other partners were Chevron's subsidiary Unocal (which was sued in a U.S. Federal Court by a group of local residents on account of the *Aliens Tort Act*; Unocal lost the case and was requested to offer substantial compensation in 2005), the Thailandese State-owned PTT company and the Myanmarese State-owned MOGE.

after a French envoy who had been sent in 2002 to assess the situation provided an overall positive assessment of the situation, Total was allowed to remain in the country.[5]

This highly mediatized case had a major impact on Total, which came to realize that the affair could seriously damage its reputation. The company intensified its CSR programs both in the region and nationwide to counter the criticism, arguing that remaining in the country would be more beneficial than leaving it. These CSR programs focused on health, education and local employment remained quite traditional even though the company made a real effort in providing tangible metrics by which to measure the impact of its action.

Total, working closely with the group Code of Ethics, also drafted an ethics charter for Myanmar. The point for the company was to show how committed it was to providing socio-economic benefits to Myanmar, while maintaining the highest possible ethical standards while operating there.

This affair also pushed Total to realize how crucial the human rights issue could be. In 2008, faced with such intense criticism and with a new CEO[6] prone to further embedding CSR into corporate practices and operations, the company started to deal with human rights from a *managerial* point of view, and no longer from a political/philanthropic one.

For the company, this meant being able to assess and measure its impacts in terms of human rights, so as to take the appropriate measures when needed. To do so, Total started to collaborate with renowned experts, working with the specialized consultancy organization Good-Corporation, which came up with recommendations on how to set up the right processes to provide the right answers. The company also decided to train several of its key managers in human rights with the help of the Danish Institute for Human Rights. This clearly indicated that for the first time, human rights were meant to be *managed*, with the help of appropriate instruments and expertise, implying a major shift in corporate culture.

---

[5] Even getting a greenlight from the French government in 2003.
[6] Christophe de Margerie, who made several public statements on the need for Total to endorse social and environmental responsibility along with its economic responsibility.

While it is impossible to measure the actual efficiency of this approach, it is clear that Total from then on was equipped with a managerial process regarding human rights. The learning experience from the Myanmar case was certainly helpful in providing the company with a better assessment of human rights-related risks[7] for future projects. In addition, the company set up a due diligence process enabling it to take corrective measures if needed. It must also be noted that Total started hiring locals to become community liaison officers, thus positioning the company to better understand the local cultural context.

An internal document published in 2009 by the General Manager of Total Myanmar E&P for investors provides evidence of this new "awareness" while of course justifying the company's decision to stay in Myanmar. Below are the concluding points:

> *"Exemplary behavior required in all aspects of our operations, especially in a country under scrutiny... Operating in a responsible manner in a country like Myanmar is possible... Successful community relations and socio-economic programs are key to our acceptability... External scrutiny and constructive criticism are positive drivers... But aggressive anti-Total campaign is counterproductive... Total committed to stay. Our presence has more positive impact than our departure".*[8]

In the wake of the Myanmar crisis, the company developed a structured human rights approach, leading it to publish a comprehensive Human Rights Guide in 2016. Even though Total does not stand out today among the firms with the very best practices in the field of human rights, it is undeniably one of the very first multinationals to recognize human rights as a CSR issue to be managed, and this put them among the earliest adopters of the new U.N. *Guiding Principles on Business and Human Rights* launched in 2011.

1.3. *The rising power of soft law*

Indeed, 2011 was a key year for the recognition of corporate responsibility in the area of human rights at a global level. First, the U.N. published its

---

[7] This was confirmed in an informal discussion with a former Ethics Director of the Group.

[8] *Total in Myanmar — Operating in a criticized country*, internal document retrieved online in 2015. Retrieved from https://www.total.com/en/myanmar

Guiding Principles on Business and Human Rights. This document provided a detailed plan for implementing the U.N. Framework established by U.N. Special Representative John Ruggie in 2008. His famous *"Protect, Respect and Remedy"* framework was the first attempt ever to articulate business responsibility with regards to human rights: *Protect* stands for the States' duty to protect civilians from human rights abuses, including those stemming from businesses. *Respect* refers to corporations' responsibility to respect human rights wherever they operate, and *Remedy* signifies the need to provide victims with access to effective remedies, both judicial and non-judicial, which means that both States and businesses are to put in place remedy mechanisms.

The *Protect, Respect and Remedy* Framework, known as the *Ruggie Principles*, has become the cornerstone of all human rights policies for corporations. The 2011 *Guiding Principles* provide a methodology for businesses wishing to develop a human rights policy as part of their CSR. The whole process revolves around the need to formalize a due diligence process, enabling companies to identify, prevent, mitigate and account for human rights abuses. This involves having the right grievance mechanisms, in order to provide practical responses. As one can see, this is far cry from the philanthropy-as-usual approach!

The emergence of a U.N.-sponsored scheme for businesses and human rights had a ripple effect on many other institutions and initiatives. Indeed, the new ISO 26000 standard on Social Responsibility released in 2010 included human rights as one of the seven Core Subjects to be addressed by organizations. Similarly, the revised *OECD Guidelines for Multinational Enterprises* added a significant section on human rights and also the obligation for member States to set up national contact points, thereby enabling them to hear and solve disputes arising from non-compliance with the OECD Guidelines. Human rights infringement quickly became one of the prominent issues handled by these contact points. Finally, the revised E.U. definition of CSR in 2011 explicitly mentioned human rights among the social and environmental concerns.[9]

This inclusion of human rights in several major international standards and guidelines represents a major turning point: From then on,

---

[9] See Chapter 1.

human rights issues were given a prominent place in the CSR agenda. This also clearly demonstrates the fact that soft law was given pride of place among all the solutions suggested. In a way it signified a retreat of international hard law in the field of business and human rights. Compliance-based CSR was deemed to be the most adequate response, pushing the CSR agenda farther from its philanthropic roots. Concretely speaking, this means that human rights from then on needed to be embedded in the CSR policies of multinationals. The question now is: What is the situation like today? Have human rights become a major dimension of the CSR policies of multinational corporations?

2. Human Rights and CSR today: Much remains to be done

The Human Rights issue has definitely become a top concern in the media today: From the Rana Plaza tragedy to the numerous reported cases of child labor, forced labor and the enslavement of migrant workers, shocking situations around the world abound. Not to mention women's rights, land rights, the displacement of indigenous peoples, lack of basic access to water and sanitation, climate change-related poverty and migrations... The scope and intensity of the human rights question continue to grow.

2.1. *Hard law advances*

The human rights issue has become such a preoccupation among Western societies that some countries have enacted legislation to minimize the risks of human rights abuses in the supply chain. Thus, the State of California passed the *Transparency in Supply Chains Act* in 2010, which compels manufacturers and retailers to publish on their websites how they "(1) engage in the verification of product supply chains to evaluate and address risks of human trafficking and slavery; (2) conduct audits of suppliers; (3) require direct supplies to certify that materials incorporated into the product comply with the laws regarding slavery and human trafficking of the countries in which they are doing business; (4) maintain accountability standards and procedures for employees or contractors that fail to meet company standards regarding slavery and human trafficking; and (5) provide employees and management training on slavery and human trafficking".[10] The main purpose of the Californian law is obviously to incite consumers to be more informed and to boycott companies practicing modern slavery and human trafficking.

In Europe, Great Britain and France have also introduced binding legislation on this subject in recent years. Great Britain passed the *Modern Slavery Act* in 2015. This law which applies to England and Wales includes a number of provisions such as the consolidation of the existing slavery and trafficking offences, the possibility for the courts to place restrictions on those convicted of modern slavery offences, the establishment of an independent Anti-slavery Commissioner and the provision of mechanisms for seizing traffickers' assets and channelling some of that money towards victims for compensation payment. It is important to note that the law does not cover human trafficking and slavery abroad, the legislator recognizes that it would be too difficult to trace them.[11]

France took a step further by voting the controversial "Duty of Care" law in 2017.[12] This law requires companies to set up a prevention plan covering the social, environmental, corruption and governance-related risks pertaining to their operations as well as to those of their subsidiaries, suppliers and subcontractors. The main aim is to enshrine human rights at the core of multinationals' responsibilities. Furthermore, the law applies to big companies with at least 5,000 employees in France. Upon request from victims, NGOs or trade unions, the courts can enjoin a company to publish a prevention plan. One must note that the financial penalties which had been foreseen for non-compliance were finally abandoned.

These recent cases of legislation on business and human rights seem to indicate that the hard law approach may still be envisaged by countries towards human rights violations. Besides, the European Union is currently examining the application of the laws in Great Britain and France which

---

[10] Retrieved from the State of California Department of Justice Website, https://oag.ca.gov/SB657.

[11] See http://www.legislation.gov.uk/ukpga/2015/30/contents/enacted

[12] *Law 2017–399 of March 27, 2017 relative to duty of care in parent companiesand ordering parties.*

is all the more urgent as the E.U. had explicitly stated that a European directive could eventually be drafted on the subject if national legislations proved effective.

This regulatory trend has had a tangible impact on multinational corporations operating in these countries. More generally speaking, it shows how important these questions have become in the Western world.

2.2. An overview of human rights policies in high risk sectors

Over the last few years, many organizations have been created to track corporate performance in the field of human rights.[13] Yet, the most recent reports show unconvincing results. The 2018 *Key Findings* from the *Corporate Human Rights Benchmark*[14] are indeed quite striking. The report was based on a multi-stakeholder consultation and company disclosure reports on 101 publicly-listed multinational corporations from Asia, Australia, Europe, North America, South America and South Africa in three strategic sectors for human rights: Apparel, agricultural goods and extractive industries.

Based on a scoring methodology (0–100%) weighting several criteria such as governance and policies, remedies and grievance mechanisms, responses to serious allegations, corporate practices and responses, and transparency, the report showed very poor performance overall. As bluntly stated in the introduction to the report:

> *"There is a race to the top in business and human rights performance, but this is only amongst a welcome cluster of leaders while the great majority have barely left the starting line"*.[15]

---

[13] See Business & Human Rights Resource Centre, https://www.business-humanrights.org/.

[14] CHRB is a non-profit company launched in 2013 and drawing expertise from seven key organisations in the field of human rights: APG Asset Management (APG), Aviva Investors, Business and Human Rights Resource Centre, The EIRIS Foundation, the Institute for Human Rights and Business (IHRB), Nordea Wealth Management and VBDO.

[15] 2018 *Key Findings* from the *Corporate Human Rights Benchmark*, p. 4.

Among the most salient features, it is worth noting that European companies score on average much higher than their counterparts, with an average score of 44% compared to 32% for South America, 22% for North America and 11% for Asia. The overall average score is 27%, with two-thirds of companies scoring below 30%.

The variations based on geographical origin are not surprising to the extent that as we saw earlier the European approach to CSR is certainly more regulation-oriented and compliance-based. In addition, the question of human rights is regulated by law in some European countries, with overall strong signals from European institutions.

But this does not mean that all European companies perform well. If one takes the top ten (scoring above 70%), one finds four European companies (Adidas, Marks & Spencer's, Unilever, and ENI), two Anglo-Australian companies (Rio Tinto and BHP Billiton), one Brazilian company (Vale) and one U.S. company (VF).

On the other hand, when one looks at the companies ranked at the bottom (scoring below 10%), one finds Chinese, Indian and Russian companies, some well-known U.S. names such as Starbucks, Kraft-Heinz or Macy's, and even more surprisingly, two European luxury brands: Prada and Hermes.

All in all, the report shows that if more and more companies tend to formalize their human rights policies, very few have set up due diligence processes, even fewer grievance mechanisms. Another striking finding is the fact that some human rights issues have been totally overlooked, such as the wages earned by workers or the protection of human rights defenders, a.k.a. "whistle-blowers". This means that virtually no companies have demonstrated strong commitments to ensure that there are living wages paid to workers in their own operations and supply chains. Furthermore, less than 10% of companies have public policy commitments concerning the protection of human rights defenders. Finally, over half of apparel and agricultural products companies are failing to honour their commitment to preventing child labour in their supply chains!

Preventing child labor does not mean that it will be possible to eradicate it right away. Moral stances are pleasing to the mind but totally inefficient, since it is well known that child labor in many poor regions around the world is fully integrated into the local economic fabric. Yet, it is multinationals' social responsibility to invest in transitory programs, whereby they finance part-time schooling of the children while striving for an objective of zero child labor in the area. This of course requires that companies closely collaborate with local governments and NGOs so that the proposed scheme is accepted by not only the community, but the parents too.

The report's findings thus show that there is still a long way to go before the large majority of multinational corporations include human rights policies in their CSR agendas. If one looks for explanations, several factors may account for this situation: First, most CSR departments are understaffed, making it very hard to correctly track human rights issues throughout the supply chain. In this respect, blockchain technology may prove to be beneficial in the near future for establishing sustainable supply chains since it will make it easier to trace the origins of all the commodities and products.

In addition, supply chain departments often remain insensitive to human rights issues. This is obviously due to the lack of specific training programs, hence the pressing need for sustainable supply chain managers today. More broadly speaking, human rights are still often viewed as a political/philanthropic issue which cannot be managed, but rather must be handled by local NGOs and through financial donations. As long as these companies do not view human rights as a risk that must be identified and managed for the sake of the whole business, human rights will remain an issue that companies consider when a crisis or a scandal erupts in the media... And in some cases, no way out is ever found, as shown by the notorious case of the Niger Delta![16]

2.3. *Best practices*

If one looks at the best practices highlighted by the 2018 report, the German sports apparel company Adidas is number one with a score exceeding 80%.[17] Second is the Anglo-Australian mining company Rio

---

[16] Oil and gas multinational Shell has, for example, been struggling with human rights problems for more than 60 years!

[17] It must be noted that Adidas was the only German company in the selected sample of 101 multinationals.

Tinto. In the case of Adidas, it is quite striking to see on their corporate website[18] that human rights are handled in detail, starting with a clear definition of the company's far-reaching human rights policy:

> *"The range of rights where we have sought to engage with governments includes discrimination, freedom of association, unlawful detention, forced labour, child labour, indigenous people's rights, and issues over livelihoods and the payment of minimum wages."*

Adidas then defines its human rights policy as a *"social obligation"*, based on a *Labor Rights Charter* and *Workplace Standards* which are an integral part of the compliance policy and the Governance structure of the company. A specific section is also dedicated to the *Modern Slavery Act*. The due diligence process *per se* is substantiated by comprehensive summaries of all the human rights cases the company has had to face since 2014, with a total of 14 cases in 2017. For each case, we are told how Adidas concretely responded, with an indication of the current status of the case, either closed, in progress or ongoing. On top of that, two remarkable initiatives must be highlighted: First, their website's very informative FAQ section on human rights, and second a dedicated third-party grievance channel open to any individual or organization wishing to file a complaint with the company.

The well-advanced integration of human rights into the CSR policy of the company is certainly due to the latter's compliance culture which is quite representative of German business culture on the whole.[19]

Furthermore, it is interesting to note that the company never uses the term CSR. Human rights are handled by the social and environmental affairs department clearly focused on a compliance approach, and under a broader umbrella, that of the sustainability strategy put forward by the company. To conclude, one can say that Adidas' strength clearly rests on its sustainability strategy, based on the triple bottom line approach, which

---

[18] Retrieved from: https://www.adidas-group.com/en/sustainability/compliance/human-rights/

[19] Including the role played by the Supervisory Board, within the German governance system of *Mitbestimmung*, especially on work-related issues.

is reflected in the strict compliance rules based on a comprehensive risk management approach.

The case of Rio Tinto which was ranked second in the report is certainly another story, that of a company faced with numerous scandals in the 1980s and 1990s, and which gradually realized how important human rights management could be in sustaining the reputational capital of the giant company in what is already a highly controversial industry, that of mining and extraction. The company has certainly learned from its mistakes, as its website communication testifies, since the human rights policy is described in a clear and comprehensive way, with a well-identified due diligence process. Nevertheless, Rio Tinto does not compare with Adidas when it comes to complaint procedures.

2.4. *The case for responsible sourcing*

Faced with mounting reputational risks, more and more multinationals are considering relocating some of their outsourced production to "safer" places. For instance, several European garment companies have relocated their subcontracting facilities to North Africa, Turkey or Eastern Europe. Some multinationals even relocate to their home country and re-internalize their production. Indeed, the higher labor costs may be recouped by more reliable quality and delivery deadlines, along with lower reputational risks. Obviously, this geographical proximity makes controlling the supply chain easier. If we take the case of Europe and its neighboring countries, social and environmental risks are likely to be much less frequent, even though the influx of migrants into Europe has sadly multiplied the number of modern slavery and human trafficking cases.[20]

At any rate, this trend does not encompass the sourcing of raw materials or agricultural commodities which are often available in only a few countries on the planet. The issue of sourcing has thus become much mediatized since an increasing number of the products we use every day contain such minerals and agricultural commodities that come from

---

[20]A shocking case was revealed recently by a French TV investigative report *Cash Investigation* (9 October 2018), that of a leather tannery in Tuscany, Italy supplying well known luxury brands and where working conditions were far from decent, with migrant workers being maltreated and exploited...

high-risk countries. For instance, most of the minerals we need for electronics goods and batteries such as cobalt, tantalum, niobium, tin and tungsten are found in the Democratic Republic of Congo, one of the most unstable and conflict-ridden countries on the planet. Watching a report on coltan mines in which children risk their lives every minute to collect the precious niobium-tantalum ore is enough to help us understand that human rights will never be respected in such cases.

Similarly, diamonds and gold are often found in African countries subject to civil war and political instability. As for the rare-earth elements necessary for many electronics goods and aerospace components, most of them come from the Inner Mongolian Province of China where social conditions are known to be appalling.

One could multiply the examples of everyday products requiring minerals and elements most likely to be extracted in violation of basic human rights. Faced with the growing international public discontent, multinationals sourcing these minerals have tried to respond by collaborating to create certification standards in conjunction with NGOs and expert groups in order to guarantee the origin of these minerals and ore.

The first mediatized case in the 1990s was that of the so-called blood diamonds extracted from war and conflict-ridden regions, mostly in Africa. The Kimberley process was set up in 2002 to guarantee the conflict-free origin of the diamonds. In subsequent years, similar types of certification appeared for gold and other minerals, like the *Responsible Jewellery Council* set up in 2005. Today, any company engaged in compliance-based CSR is likely to adhere to these certification schemes.

Unfortunately, several reports and enquiries confirm the fact that these well-intentioned processes are far from reliable. Through corruption and the extremely complex chains of intermediaries, it is currently virtually impossible to ascertain that the certification is an effective guarantee. Multinationals are becoming increasingly aware of the fact that these types of engagements are not sufficient, and that more and more investigations prove that these schemes are totally flawed, which in turn reinforces the consumers' apprehensions that CSR is nothing but green- and social-washing!

The next step requires that companies spend significantly more time and resources working directly on the ground with reliable suppliers in long-term partnerships, and eventually acquire and fully operate operations in order to exert direct control over the human rights issues.

In this respect, an interesting initiative was taken by the Dutch smartphone company Fairphone which launched in 2013 the first ethical smartphone, i.e. produced in the best social and environmental conditions possible all along the value chain, with an innovative design, after-sales service and a circular approach.[21] Concerning the critical minerals sourcing phase, Fairphone has engaged in long-term projects with selected suppliers from such high-risk countries as Congo, Uganda and Indonesia. Instead of fleeing from high-risk countries such as the Democratic Republic of Congo, Fairphone is constantly striving to set up innovative long-term partnerships there, backed by local foundations to progress towards responsible sourcing and mining. Though a very small player in a large market, Fairphone manages to show that it is possible to produce a smartphone with minimized social and environmental risks. The more its products are sold (there are currently around 100,000 Fairphone owners around the world), the more the company will be in a position to entice the major players in the industry to adopt new practices and pay closer attention to the sourcing of minerals.

The same challenge applies to agricultural commodities, with the emblematic cases of palm oil and cotton among many others. Certification schemes have also been set up, such as the *Better Cotton Initiative* in 2005 and the *Roundtable on Sustainable Palm Oil* in 2004. In the same way, several reports have pointed out the very limited results of these initiatives which remain socially and environmentally vague and poorly monitored.

Nevertheless, one of the best current practices in the field of responsible sourcing is actually related to agricultural commodities: French natural beauty products and organic cosmetics company L'Occitane en Provence, and its sourcing of shea butter in Sub-Saharan Burkina Faso.

2.4.1. *L'Occitane in Burkina Faso*

French company L'Occitane en Provence is an impressive success story known worldwide, with sales skyrocketing globally, especially in Asia.

---

[21] See next chapter on circular economy.

The company was founded in 1976 by Olivier Bassan, whose idea was to make products from natural ingredients obtained in a socially responsible way. When Mr Bassan visited Burkina Faso in the early 1980s, he discovered the incredible cosmetic properties of shea butter, known as "women's gold" there, since this nut produced from an endemic species is harvested exclusively by women.

Olivier Bassan decided to start working directly with five women's cooperatives which would provide him with semi-artisanal shea butter, a decision which incidentally made L'Occitane a pioneer in the Western world for the use of shea butter in cosmetics. What is remarkable is the fact that the company continued to buy from these cooperatives despite the numerous difficulties they encountered in subsequent years; indeed, they were faced with major quality and transportation problems: Burkina Faso is a landlocked country, and storing, packing and transporting the shea butter in proper conditions proved quite challenging. In addition, the quality of the butter was very irregular. This did not discourage L'Occitane, and on the contrary the company kept developing its shea butter products and thus bought more and more from the cooperatives while gradually contributing to helping the women improve their production and management skills. Today, L'Occitane is the biggest direct buyer of shea butter, with annual purchases that can sometimes go up to 750 tons![22]

The L'Occitane Foundation created in 2006 aimed to increase the social benefits of the shea butter business. Substantial amounts of money have been dedicated to finance literacy and capacity building programs since then. The next major step was taken in 2009 with the fairtrade certification process of all the cooperatives working with L'Occitane backed up with financial and technical support from the company. L'Occitane also realized it needed to collaborate with reliable partners who could help it make the best decisions; they thus engaged in a partnership with the highly reputed Canadian non-profit organization Centre for International Studies and Cooperation (CECI).

Today, nearly 100% of the shea butter bought by L'Occitane is fair trade certified, which manifests in a 30% premium on the selling price compared to the local market. On top of that, 2% of all sales proceeds go

---

[22] From L'Occitane's Supply chain report, July 2016.

to social development fund aimed at financing long-term community development projects. Prepayment has also grown over the years, representing 80% today. Both provide the cooperatives with a strong protection from potential hazards and an opportunity to invest if needed. The contracts with the cooperatives are renewable three-year contracts while the buying price is revised annually by a multi-stakeholder committee.

The sourcing policy of L'Occitane was singled out in 2013 by the UNDP which described it as "exemplary".[23] Indeed, what must be highlighted is the genuine long-term commitment of the company, which has lasted for more than three decades now, and the fact that shea butter is bought directly from the cooperatives, not through intermediaries (the most common schema), and which inevitably entails a drop in the final remuneration for the women![24] It must be added that having chosen to buy semi-artisanal shea butter may represent an extra cost for L'Occitane (the butter is further refined in the Netherlands), but at the same time this enables the women to remain independent and to maintain a more traditional approach, not disrupting the local culture around shea trees.

Thus, L'Occitane truly has a tangible positive impact on women's empowerment as it works directly with them. It is estimated that this benefits more than 10,000 women today. It is also interesting to point out that the L'Occitane Foundation is a strong support structure which provides further social benefits that the responsible purchasing contracts do not cover. In this case, philanthropy serves as a direct tool supporting business, which is positively meaningful and impactful.

It goes without saying that this policy is grounded in the company's DNA since its very positioning is based on natural ingredients which have been sourced sustainably. From a practical perspective, a team of three officers work full time at the head office on the Burkina Faso shea butter supply; they undertake at least four trips per year in the field and work with local consultants all year round.

---

[23] See report *"L'Occitane au Burkina Faso", More than just business with shea butter producers*, Yarri Kamak, UNDP, retrieved on line, http://www.undp.org/content/dam/undp/library/corporate/Partnerships/Private%20Sector/AFIMcases/UNDP%20GIM%20Case%20Study%20LOccitane%20Final.pdf

[24] Such is the case for L'Oréal, another major buyer today.

From a business standpoint, L'Occitane enjoys a competitive advantage, since it definitely was a first mover in Western countries. Today it sells more than 100 products containing shea butter among which some of its flagship products. Let us not underestimate the fact that the high margins in this line of business make it easier to invest in responsible sourcing policies.

There are, of course, some risks and limitations. First, this unique partnership has made a lot of women dependent on one single client, which is why L'Occitane has been pushing cooperatives to diversify their clients. Indeed, what if the company went out of business? Also, the fact of maintaining semi-artisanal techniques, while being beneficial from a socio-economic perspective, proves much less positive for the environment since the techniques used necessitate a lot of wood burning, thus contributing to deforestation and air pollution. L'Occitane is currently working on this issue, trying to find more environment-friendly techniques.

Lastly, the issue of increasing the economic value of the shea butter is another cause for concern: L'Occitane is indeed aware of it, and they have launched interesting initiatives to help develop production facilities locally. Thus, some local manufacturers are regularly invited to the L'Occitane production facilities in Southern France and trained for a few months there. In addition, L'Occitane regularly launches campaigns in its stores during which shea butter soap made in Burkina Faso is sold. But this is always for a limited period of time, and one may wonder why L'Occitane does not go further in helping the African country develop its own industry, which would of course contribute to long-term economic development. But after all, L'Occitane is a commercial buyer, and in no case a development agency…

Be that as it may, the L'Occitane case does prove that sourcing may be done in a responsible way, which here does not mean "less harmful or risky" regarding human rights, but clearly contributes to improving human rights, in this case the rights of women in one of the poorest countries on the planet.

But this also means that this type of social business is done with a purpose, long-term vision and commitment, and on a relatively small scale. In other words, could such successful procurement policies be possible within multinationals that deal with thousands of producers in tens of countries around the world and put hundreds of products on the market? This is a crucial question that takes us beyond CSR, but which needs to be raised here: Our guess is that *big* is probably not *beautiful* when it comes to sustainable and responsible business...

As we saw in the previous chapter on employee representation, the question of human rights also demonstrates how intricate the social side of CSR is in our open globalized world. This is certainly due to the fact that CSR was largely inspired by a philanthropy-based approach, and that social issues were almost entirely focused on giving back to the community, including to the company's employees.

Furthermore, seen from our European perspective, the debate over the position of CSR vis-à-vis regulation remains open, and even questions the very relevance of "social CSR". The answer certainly lies in the necessary shift of social CSR from a traditional philanthropic view to a sustainability-driven and innovative form. As we will see in the following chapter, sustainability appeared long after CSR was born, and today is mostly associated with environmental issues.

Yet, in our opinion, the future of CSR clearly depends on whether the difficult but necessary convergence between the social and environmental challenges of sustainability will eventually be reached. In other words, contributing as a company to a planet where people everywhere live decently and sustainably in a sustainable environment, both globally and locally.

CHAPTER 5

FROM CSR TO SUSTAINABILITY — LEARNING FROM NATURE

As we have observed, the concept of CSR is complex, given the various interpretations behind it. If I were to ask millenials what CSR is, they would certainly cite the environment first. Yet, for several decades CSR did not explicitly focus on the environment, even though Bowen did have some visionary insights into environmental issues. In the same way, CSR for most of the world today is associated with community-related actions, i.e. human-centered priorities... which seems meaningful for developing countries whose governments lack the means or the will to provide their people with decent living and working conditions.

Millenials would still put the environment as a top priority on the CSR agenda because they were born and raised at a time when sustainable development was an established concept. Indeed, since 1987 and the Brundtland report, sustainable development has become a major political and economic issue with global outreach.

Nonetheless, it took some time before sustainable development actually reached out to the business world. It was initially clearly designed as a diplomatic concept, 15 years after the first U.N. Stockholm conference on the Human Environment. Even though the 1992 Rio Declaration did include businesses among the relevant stakeholders, it was only in 2002 at the Johannesburg Summit that CEOs from top Western multinationals took part and committed to integrating sustainability concerns in their companies.

Since then, sustainable development has been ever more connected to business responsibility: This chapter will examine how sustainability

111

gradually entered into corporate strategies and policies to eventually become a strategic key for the future. To illustrate this, we will conclude this chapter by focusing on what we consider to be one of the better examples, if not the best: That of U.S. carpet manufacturer Interface Inc., which we have been following for the last 20 years.

1. CSR and sustainability: From environmental compliance to opportunity

Sustainability was and still is to some extent associated with environmental issues. Indeed, the sustainable development concept is clearly rooted in the ecological imperative, i.e. the growing awareness of the limits of our development model based on infinite resources and unlimited growth. Supported by scientific findings, the Brundtland report's first aim was to propose an alternative development model which would take into account the longer-term impact of our activities on the planet and its fragile ecosystems.

Whereas some pioneer companies such as The Body Shop and Ben & Jerry's had already committed to sustainable strategies as early as the late 1970s, businesses really started to take into account the consequences of their activities on the environment only during the 1990s. The Body Shop and Ben & Jerry's were, and still are, pioneer companies which put sustainability objectives at the core of their visions. They were among some of the first so-called "purpose-driven" companies whose founders prioritized environmental and/or social causes, or as they put it themselves, "militant capitalism".[1]

Both cases remain valid today in the sense that they came up with groundbreaking innovative practices, from ethical/environmental sourcing policies to the constant search for social (Ben & Jerry's) and environmental (The Body Shop) performance. But these cases were limited to a small number of companies created by visionary sustainability-driven people.[2] Mainstream business had not really moved on the topic in the 1980s!

---

[1] See for instance, CEO of The Body Shop Anita Roddick's book *Business as Unusual*, 2005.
[2] One could mention the French companies Natures et Découvertes and L'Occitane.

The first companies to embrace environmental concerns were either pushed to do so by local institutional pressure or because of sectorial issues. Thus, manufacturing industries relying on heavy inputs of raw materials and energy started to pay heed to their environmental impact, developing new tools (such as life cycle analyses) aimed at minimizing their negative impacts on the environment, introducing the "environmental footprint" concept, and also providing savings on raw materials and energy consumption. This was the case in the 1980s for several Japanese and Northern European companies: Japan, as to be expected, was naturally sensitive to resource scarcity. For similar reasons, Northern European countries were pioneers in terms of environmental regulation and incentives. They were followed by other European, U.S. and Anglo-Saxon companies out of mimetic pressure.

Thus, from the 1990s to the 2000s, sustainability was by and large associated with environmental policies focused on impact minimization approaches. Environmental economics was starting to develop, providing economic instruments that helped companies to cut costs while contributing to a better environment. In the European Union, this trend was obviously backed up by extensive environmental regulations. The same applied to some extent to Japan and some parts of the U.S.[3] Obviously, most companies around the world were still either ignoring environmental issues or only adhering to minimum compliance with the law. Some multinationals at that time also engaged in partnerships with international NGOs seeking advice, technical assistance and reputation enhancement.[4]

1.1. Moving beyond compliance

1.1.1. *The rise of environmental sustainability awareness*

Some authors developed models showing the various stages of the sustainability journey for businesses, thereby adopting a business case approach,

---

[3]The State of California, for instance, was granted a waiver, meaning that it is allowed to legislate on its own. Californian environmental legislation today is far more ambitious and far-reaching than its federal counterpart.

[4]See Chapter 2.

Figure 9:   Willard's 5-step sustainability journey

in other words, aiming to prove that sustainability is ultimately a business opportunity. If we take Willard's 5-stage sustainability journey model,[5] this growing awareness among businesses of the necessity to mitigate the negative impacts on the environment is clearly associated with its Phase 3, "Beyond compliance", when companies realize the need to move further than simply complying with the law.

At Stage 3, the main drivers for companies are eco-efficiency, i.e. cost savings generated by resource cuts, reputational risk and regulatory threats, especially in the anticipation of new legislation. Companies then start to adopt environmental management systems, such as ISO 14001 with a view to reducing their use of resources (water, energy, etc.) and cutting down on waste following the famous 3Rs, "Reduce, Reuse and Recycle". The measures taken are usually closely related both to the local regulatory environment and to consumer pressure. In developed countries, companies may focus on packaging weight reduction, while in developing countries the priority might be switching to LED lighting. Besides, integrating environmental concerns enables businesses to

---

[5] Willard, 2007.

anticipate future legal requirements and to communicate on their environmental commitments. But environmental communication may prove tricky especially at a stage when the measures taken are partial and not systematic as we will see below.

Nidumolu *et al.* in their 2009 paper[6] also identified five stages of the sustainability journey, while focusing on the necessary convergence between sustainability and innovation.

"Moving beyond compliance" definitely corresponds to Phase 1, "compliance as opportunity" i.e. when companies realize that reducing the company's environmental footprint may turn into an opportunity for innovation, growth and possibly value creation. Companies then start to invest in cleaner technologies which are expected to bring a positive return in the medium term.

Moving beyond compliance gradually prompted companies to develop environmental "strategies" aimed at providing them with comparative advantages. In this respect, the 2006 Orsato approach provides a relevant model. Orsato entitled his paper *"When does it pay to be green?".*[7] The objective is clear. In his matrix, he identified four main types of strategies based either on cost or differentiation and applying to either processes or products/services.

Figure 10: Nidumolu *et al.*'s 5-step to sustainability

---

[6] Nidumolu, R., Prahalad, C. K., & Rangaswami, M. R.: "Why Sustainability is Now the Key Driver of Innovation", *Harvard Business Review*, 87(9) 2009, pp. 56–64.
[7] Orsato, R.J.: "Competitive Environmental Strategies: When does it Pay to be Green?, *California Management Review*, 2006.

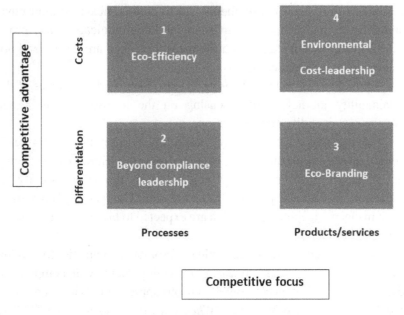

Figure 11:   Orsato's environmental strategy matrix

By integrating environmental awareness into their products and/or processes, companies started to acquire a new mindset enabling them to link environmental objectives with performance. For instance, setting up environmental indicators and reporting on them brought companies closer to the triple bottom line approach devised by Elkington,[8] or at least to a "dual bottom line" linking environmental and economic performance.

Thus, CSR has been upholding sustainability mainly through environmental concerns. But this has been a gradual process first concerning big impact industries under pressure from various external factors such as institutional environments, industry trends or consumer expectations. But once again the approach has remained, up until recently, largely reactive, aimed at reducing negative impacts, which tended to be more correlated to mitigating risks.

Today, this "beyond compliance" stage is still the prevailing approach to the environment. All sectors are gradually adopting it, since the

---

[8] See Chapter 1.

environmental pillar clearly appears to be a mandatory dimension of CSR today. This phenomenon is especially noticeable in the case of services. The same trend applies to the developing world where major local companies and foreign subsidiaries are starting to develop CSR actions related to the environmental dimension. The growing awareness of the 17 U.N. Sustainable Development Goals is surely largely responsible for this recent evolution.

Companies therefore use the term sustainability more and more often in their CSR discourse. This tends to generate some additional confusion about the scope of CSR and that of sustainability, and does not really contribute to building up a transparent and positive image of CSR since many environmental measures are viewed as mere greenwashing tactics by the general public.

Another confusing issue is that of the voluntary dimension of sustainability-driven CSR: Many companies tend to purposely blur the line between legal requirements and voluntary measures taken for the environment. This is striking in the case of the European Union where many companies tend to overplay their voluntary contributions to environmental responsibility when in actual fact many of their policies are required by law.

Yet, it is clear today that a substantial number of medium- and large-sized companies around the world are no longer ignoring environmental issues. Globalization and the spread of international standards and frameworks have certainly contributed to this. At the same time, most of these companies still view the environment as an additional constraint to take into account, as an obligation towards society, but certainly not as an opportunity for a new vision and strategy.

1.1.2. Social sustainability, the missing link?

Whereas sustainability is most often associated with the ecological imperative, the social pillar needs to be fully considered. Yet, the social dimension of sustainability remains by and large unclearly defined and poorly handled. As we saw earlier, today's CSR practices around the world are still dominated by philanthropy; on the other hand, the internal social dimension of CSR is struggling hard to exist as such. This creates a desequilibrium to the extent that very few companies actually engage in a genuine triple bottom line approach which would give equal importance to social and environmental performance issues. Moreover, measuring social performance remains much harder than for the environment since it has much to do with local cultural and regulatory norms which vary considerably from one country to another. Thus, quantifying the impact of socially focused CSR policies is a major challenge today.

Yet, more and more companies are devising social sustainability policies. These can take the form of innovative socially inclusive businesses[9] or programs aimed at fostering human capital through talent and diversity management, employability and wellbeing at work. These voluntary employee-related policies are often found in developed countries where the level of social regulation remains high. Companies in the developing world, on the other hand, often struggle to provide basic benefits to their employees and still view CSR as "repackaged" philanthropy. Despite some promising evolutions, one can undoubtedly assert that sustainability-driven CSR is primarily concerned with environmental considerations. The convergence between environmental and social sustainability will definitely remain a key objective for the years to come.

1.2. Learning from nature: Embedding sustainability

The main challenge today is to embed sustainability into corporate vision and strategy. This requires adopting a brand-new mindset which in the end stresses the positive role of business toward the natural environment. This presupposes a radical departure from today's dominant economic models, which will ultimately lead to a total reassessment and redesign of business models.

1.2.1. The climate "push"

The move to environmental embeddedness has assuredly been gaining momentum lately. It is the case for several large multinationals operating in big impact industries, especially in the European Union. Indeed, the E.U. has been pushing its environmental agenda for businesses for the last 15 years,

---

[9] See Chapter 6.

moving from "command-and-control" policies to "smart" market-based regulations and incentives.

Thus, the focus on climate emerged relatively early in the E.U. For instance, even though its efficiency remains to be seen, the emissions trading scheme launched in 2005 had a tangible impact on the companies involved. While one may still question its efficiency today, this innovative market approach did help internalize CO_2[10] by giving it a price on the market. This "psychological" effect remains, in my opinion, the only tangible achievement of this scheme. It clearly contributed to internalizing environmental issues by "commodifying" them.

Over the last decade, the round of global climate summits culminating with the COP 21 Paris conference in 2015 have played a decisive role in the fight against climate change: In Paris, several large multinationals took part in the discussions and formally committed to cutting their greenhouse gas emissions, thus agreeing to do their share. In this respect, the COP 21 conference appears to have been a turning point. Interestingly enough, several major U.S. companies such as General Electric, Walmart, Ford and Mars strongly reacted against the Trump Administration's 2017 decision to withdraw from the Paris Agreement. These companies announced that they would maintain their environmental commitments to the climate. In short, rising global climate awareness definitely contributed to embedding environmental sustainability issues into the corporate strategies and policies of more and more multinationals.

1.2.2. *Toward an integrated approach*

The climate focus demonstrates an ongoing shift among businesses towards a more integrated approach to sustainability. More and more companies are reaching Willard's "integrated strategy" phase. This requires that companies adopt a comprehensive value chain approach to sustainability which will eventually lead to transforming value propositions and business models.[11] Concretely speaking, this implies setting up sustainability objectives

---

[10] The use of CO_2 here refers to both CO_2 and CO_2 equivalents from man-made greenhouse gases.

[11] See Chapter 1, Porter & Kramer, 2006.

validated by top management and encompassing the entire value chain from the R&D phase to the product's end of life.

This difficult move requires shifting from a sustainability approach mostly triggered by constraint and image to a radical change through which sustainability is fully embedded in the corporate vision and strategy. To illustrate this mindset shift, let us review the case of a company making consumer products for the general public. Due to growing consumer pressure, the company may be urged to develop one green product; It will then strive to obtain an ecolabel. Offering such a "green" product in its line will be the company's response to consumer expectations. At this point, the company's strategy is responsive. One product is available for environmentally conscious consumers while the other products remain the same.

If the company were to decide to set up a strategic plan aimed at drastically reducing the environmental footprint of all of its products, its environmental strategy would become proactive and strategically embedded. But the company is then likely to be faced with two overwhelming challenges. The first one is that of the supply chain, especially if it has been outsourced. Indeed, how will the company be able to talk its suppliers into adopting its strategy? What if for cost-cutting reasons. most of the suppliers are located in developing countries where social and environmental challenges abound?[12]

The second challenge, which is less debated today in academic literature on CSR, but is a major operational concern for companies is that of the marketing department and their readiness to adopt the environmental strategy and really "play the game". Empirical studies show that marketers tend to resist sustainability-related changes since they still largely believe that such "green" products do not sell. This leads us to believe that one of the keys to implementing sustainability strategies today is a much-needed cultural revolution in the world of marketing. This implies rethinking the whole marketing mix and more generally the brand strategy. Our experience suggests that B2B companies with a narrower range of products are likely to be "better off" when it comes to the implementation

---

[12] See the *Rana Plaza* case discussed earlier.

phase. The case of the Interface company which we will discuss in depth in the second section of this chapter is a perfect illustration of this.

As I write these lines, Apple has just announced the launch of its first 100% recycled aluminum laptop. For a company whose iconic former CEO Steve Jobs did not seem to care too much about e-waste up until NGOs such as Greenpeace attacked Apple for its poor environmental record, this is a major leap forward. I see it as evidence of an acceleration process involving several major companies which are for various reasons moving to integrated strategies leading to the reshuffling of business models. This recent trend is largely due to the growing awareness that our current economic model has become unsustainable and that it is high time we learned from the natural world around us to become truly sustainable for the future generations.

1.3. Learning from Nature

What is currently at stake in this major mindset shift is the emergence of a new way of considering our economic and industrial processes. The sustainability revolution seems to be underway because the business world has started to radically question how it is impacting the planet and now is striving to find appropriate solutions.

It all started with the realization that our development model (which is based on modern European philosophical thinking and was first deployed by the Industrial Revolution in England in the 18th and 19th centuries) is leading us into a dead end. Indeed, the idea that we can indefinitely take from the Earth, produce more and more without caring about what happens when our products are not used any longer is outdated and dangerous. For too long we have followed a linear approach to production following a *take-make-waste* pattern and this is the main cause of our "unsustainability" today.

Several economists started to radically question our unsustainable economic development model as early as the 1950s and 1960s,[13] focusing

---

[13] See for instance what was later known as *ecological economics* with Georgescu-Roegen and his bioeconomics, Daly and his steady growth theory or Kenneth Boulding and his evolutionary economics. One of the most influential representatives of ecological economics today is Robert Costanza.

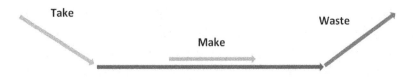

Figure 11:   The linear production-consumption pattern

on the finite dimension of our world and its resources. Such was the case, for instance, for the famous essay comparing our Earth to a spaceship written by Kenneth Boulding in 1966, which inspired the 1972 Club of Rome report *Limits to Growth.*[14]

Alternative economic sustainability approaches gained popularity in the 1990s in the wake of the Rio Summit and other major international commitments which started to emerge. Among all these alternative approaches, the school of *Natural Capitalism* played a decisive role in bridging the gap between business and the need to radically rethink our economic model. Indeed, while the ecological economics movement and its theoretical questionings about the concept of growth, progress and exploitation of natural resources did have a major impact on defining economic sustainability, their conclusions are not easily transferable to our world as it is, where capitalism has become the only economic system currently in force.

Natural capitalism on the other hand provides an attempt to reconcile our market-based economies with a radical reengineering of our production and consumption models. Born in the U.S. in the 1980s, the theory of natural capitalism has been developed not by economists, but by environmentalists and scientists such as Paul Hawken, Amory and Hunter Lovins.[15] Whereas some may rightly think that embedding sustainability implies finding an alternative to capitalism, the natural capitalism approach is based on a realistic assessment, that of the overwhelming penetration of market-based economies. Yet, its vision presupposes a total mindset change based on the acute observation of natural mechanisms.

---

[14] Dennis & Donatella Meadows *et al.*
[15] Founders of the renowned *Rocky Mountain Institute* in the 1980s.

The key argument behind natural capitalism is that we all have before our eyes an amazing example of a sustainable production and consumption model, that of the natural world and its ecosystems. Indeed, when one observes the biological realities of Nature, three main dimensions of this "natural capital" stand out:

1) A limited stock of resources, many of which are not renewable. Considering renewable sources, our current footprint is so large they will not suffice soon.
2) Ecosystems are inspiring models based on exchanges of material and energy flows. They are closed-loop mechanisms such as a forest ecosystem.
3) Essential services are provided to humankind for free. These so-called ecosystem services have never been "counted" yet. Among these services, one finds the provision of food, raw materials and water of course but also regulating services like pollination (bees and other insects), climate regulation and carbon sequestration (oceans and forests) or water purification (wetlands). One may even add recreational services such as spiritual and aesthetic fulfillment or outdoor activities.

The main principle of natural capitalism implies a complete reversal of perspective: Instead of submitting natural capital to the economy, the time has come to organize the economy around the biological/ecological realities of Nature. This requires focusing on a drastic increase in resource efficiency to provide humans with sustainable wellbeing. It is important at this point to add that natural capitalism does not overlook the social and human dimensions of sustainability. On the contrary, social justice is its other key objective. Thus, organizing the economy around the ecological imperative has to go hand in hand with providing material wellbeing to the greatest number and redressing inequalities.

Natural capitalism has given way to a series of new approaches and tools developed over the last 25 years. These all aim at radically redesigning the production process so that ultimately we will not have to take any more from the planet nor discharge into it, leading to what is now known as the circular economy.

At the corporate level, circular economy approaches aim at closing the loop, i.e. eliminating the notion of waste which instead becomes a resource, such as secondary raw materials for example. Eliminating waste may be achieved by focusing on the production stage, through eco-efficiency and ecodesign approaches. To do so, life cycle assessment (LCA) tools have been developed to measure the impact of a product throughout its life cycle, from "cradle" (energy and raw materials) to "grave" (end of life of the product). LCAs have become commonplace in the last few years. With the circular economy, the aim is obviously to move towards "cradle-to-cradle".[16]

The circular economy approach also requires extending the producer's responsibility: indeed, the entire value chain must be taken into account, i.e. upstream into the supply chain and downstream after the end of life of the product. One key challenge today is therefore to manage to "bring on board" suppliers and subcontractors and to extend the life of the product through recovery, reuse and/or recycling operations.

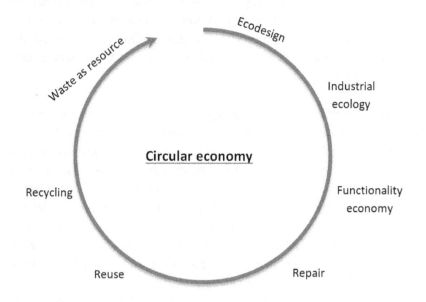

Figure 12:   The circular economy process

---

[16] See Braungart & McDonough, *Cradle to Cradle: Remaking the Way We Make Things* (2002).

Other options like dematerialization may also contribute: by choosing to offer a service/solution instead of selling a product, not only are the companies innovating from a business and marketing perspective, but this also helps them manage and reduce their impact on the environment, since they produce less and thus take less energy and raw materials from the planet. The revenue they lose from selling less may compensated by the additional services offered (maintenance, etc.). The circular approach indeed fosters the search for longer product life spans. Thus, repair and maintenance become new selling arguments.

The case of the U.S. outdoor wear company Patagonia is emblematic. Known as a unique model in the fashion industry of a company aiming to be truly sustainable, the Californian brand founded by iconic Yvon Chouinard[17] in the 1970s is famous for its engagement both in the traceability of its supply chain as well as its policy focusing on increasing the lifespan of its clothes. In a famous advertising campaign for Black Friday in 2011, the company adopted a radical stance by advertising one of its products in major national newspapers with the following tagline: *"Don't buy this jacket!"*. The idea behind this provocative message was to promote Patagonia's *Common Threads* initiative, the aim of which was to convince its customers to extend the lifespan of their products by offering repair services or encouraging them to share and exchange their gear with others. Accused by many of hypocritically creating a buzz to sell more, the company, whose sales actually boomed during Black Friday, decided in 2016 to donate all of its Black Friday profits to charities.

At the territorial level, the field of industrial ecology has been steadily growing over the years. The main reason for this being to create an industrial ecosystem in which all the entities are interdependent and in which are exchanged flows of matter and/or energy just like in a natural ecosystem. A famous pioneer experiment of what is also known as ecological symbiosis is that of the Kalundborg eco-industrial park in Denmark. Created as early as 1972, this private park is the most complete symbiosis in existence today with over 30 exchanges of waste, water and materials between a power plant, and public and private companies. To provide just

---

[17] See Chouinard's book, *Let My People Go Surfing: The Education of a Reluctant Businessman* (2006).

a few examples, the heat generated by the power plant becomes a source of heating for private homes, the sludge is turned into fertilizer for a fish farm, the steam is sold to pharmaceutical company Novo Nordisk, by-products such as gypsum are sold to a manufacturing company, while ash and clinker are used for road surfacing or to make cement. This unique case has generated impressive environmental and economic benefits; regarding environmental impact, the Kalundborg park has obviously made it possible to drastically reduce inputs of energy and raw materials as well as discharges of waste into the environment.

Applying natural processes to manufacturing and industry is clearly the new industrial revolution we need to build up a sustainable and responsible world. Yet, concrete commercial applications remain scarce today. Many companies are indeed moving into the circular economy, but most of them are still testing circular approaches: they invest in the development of new ecodesigned products, strive to increase the recycling rate of their products, but still stick to mainstream approaches, fearing to move into unknown territory which could prove dangerous in terms of sales and revenues. This is clearly the case in B2B industries such as cement, manufacturing, energy, mining as well as in highly mediatized B2C industries such as fashion, agribusiness, or food and beverage. Interesting examples abound, from Lafarge to Coca Cola, from H&M to Danone, but their impacts still remain marginal from an operational perspective.

Corporate leaders tend to blame it on the high investment costs involved. If there are for sure financial obstacles, the main challenge today is the change in mindset, from R&D to marketing. A lot has to do with corporate values and how they can be made to trigger change and innovation. In this respect, employee involvement and active participation is a prerequisite to any successful outcome.

An interesting example is provided by German company BASF and its *Verbund* principle. This principle pushed by top management is based on the idea of putting together production plants, energy and waste flows, logistics and infrastructure so as to reach drastic improvements in economic efficiency and environmental impact. Currently implemented in six production sites around the world wih impressive results, this innovative circular approach emanating from an old industrial giant does give room for hope in the ability of the manufacturing sector to move toward sustainability.

1.3.1. *New challenges*

Product "re-entry"

Whereas the circular economy aims at minimizing inputs from the Earth and outputs into the environment, ultimately leading to zero waste, awareness is growing today over the exponential increase in non degradable waste discharged into our environment. One major concern today is clearly that of plastic: its accumulation in the oceans with the notorious "garbage sea" is having multiple disastrous effects on biodiversity, marine life and water contamination. It may be ingested by fish and sea mammals, and its disintegration process leaks toxic elements into water and marine life, etc. As pointed out in a report published by the World Economic Forum and the Ellen MacArthur Foundation,[18] the weight of plastic in the sea could exceed the total weight of fish in the oceans by 2050!

Faced with this unsustainable prospect, some companies are starting to react and come up with ways of collecting the plastic from the ocean so as to reintroduce it into their manufacturing processes. By having plastic "re-enter" the economic loop, companies manage to limit their inputs from raw materials while having a positive impact on the natural environment. Such is the case of the *Parley for the Oceans* project in which the German company Adidas is involved. Working toward *"finding ways to synchronize the economic system of humankind with the ecosystem"*,[19] Adidas has been able to produce shoes made from ocean plastic. If the program at the beginning was viewed rather as greenwashing, given the extremely limited number of shoes produced, the company has since managed to develop it commercially to a larger scale. One million pairs of shoes were sold in 2017, the goal being to reach five million in 2018. Could we ever have imagined that all Adidas shoes will be made from ocean plastic in a few years from now? There is surely enough plastic in the oceans to provide Adidas with enough secondary raw materials for quite some time...

---

[18] *The New Plastic Economy — Rethinking the future of plastics* (2016).
[19] Retrieved from https://www.parley.tv

1.3.2. *Imitating nature: Biomimicry*

Nature is an endless source of inspiration for businesses to innovate sustainably: this is the key principle of the biomimicry approach which appeared about 25 years ago. Founded by U.S. biologist Janine Benyus,[20] biomimicry urges us to identify those principles and strategies developed by living organisms and ecosystems which will help us live sustainably and in harmony with the natural environment.

Biomimicry operates at various levels from simple imitation of shapes and materials such as the hook-and-loop fasteners known as *Velcro* which were inspired from burdock to spider silk that is reproduced in an industrial way. Another level of biomimicry is that of *in vitro* reproduction of natural mechanisms, involving sophisticated processes. However, the most potentially impactful level is undoubtedly the still under-developed replication of mature natural ecosystems which will enable us to create sustainable human ecosystems based on cooperation strategies. The "Ten Commandments" proclaimed by Benyus to accomplish this are very similar to the circular economy principles. Biomimicry is a promising approach whose potential is far from being fulfilled.

One may wonder at this point what the link with CSR is. Aren't we talking about purely business and industrial innovation? Although the number of companies becoming involved in circular approaches remains quite limited, this emerging trend is certainly closely related to sustainability-driven CSR or, in other words, the strategic embeddedness of CSR. It is indeed only when key CSR issues have been embedded in the corporate vision and strategies that such industrial strategies can be deployed. As shown by Nidumolu *et al.*, companies have then reached the ultimate stage of sustainability-driven innovation leading them to rethink their business models. In a nutshell, CSR may indeed be the driving force behind radical innovations and systemic change.

Coming back to the theoretical debate discussed in the first chapter of this book, we firmly believe that the greatest potential development of CSR lies in holistic sustainability-driven strategies that will bring about radical value chain transformations. This is clearly a more

---

[20] Janine Benyus, *Biomimicry: Innovation Inspired by Nature* (2002).

European perspective, quite distinct from Porter & Kramer's emphasis on strategic philanthropy. This does not mean, of course, that there are no U.S. companies among those implementing the best practices today; it is quite the contrary. But these companies such as Patagonia or Interface are driven by a unique entrepreneurial vision, rather than broader institutional pressure.

In any case, learning from Nature is more crucial than ever for businesses: in a world faced with an acceleration of climate change and such a rapid loss of biodiversity that scientists now talk of a "sixth wave of extinction", the private sector has a major role to play in contributing to finding the appropriate answers to the sustainability challenge.

From reducing their negative impacts and aiming at a zero negative impact on the environment, businesses must now turn to a greater challenge: being able to restore and regenerate the environment. This is the unique strategy adopted by the U.S. carpet tile manufacturer Interface that we shall now examine in detail.

2. Interface, a model sustainable company?[21]

Unknown to the general public, Interface is a U.S. company founded in the 1970s, based in Atlanta, Georgia. The inventor of the carpet tile, Interface is the world leader in modular flooring. A relatively small multinational listed on the NASDAQ stock market, it has 3,300 employees, operates in 110 countries, with five production facilities in Europe, the U.S., Thailand and Australia and an annual turnover of around one billion dollars.

The case of Interface is quite unique since the company which at first had no connection whatsoever with sustainability has become a worldwide reference with over 20 years of experience in sustainability embeddedness. Indeed, the "sustainability journey" as it was dubbed by its charismatic founder Ray Anderson started in 1994.

---

[21] For this chapter on the Interface company, I am indebted to several people at Interface who were of great help in providing insights and information along the years. My gratitude goes to founder and CEO, the late Ray Anderson, and to Laure Rondeau-Desroches and Geanne van Arkel.

2.1 *How it all started*

In 1994, Ray Anderson was asked by some clients to deliver a speech on what Interface was doing for the environment. As Anderson explained later on,[22] he realized his company was doing nothing at all, apart from being compliant with the law. Anderson then was given the chance to read Paul Hawken's book *The Ecology of Commerce*. Reading this book was what he described later as an "epiphany", a true revelation which from then on pushed him to embark his company on a radical turnaround with sustainability embedded at the core of the business.

The company's journey towards sustainability was thus triggered by a vision, a new purpose: as Anderson explained, the point was not to stop producing carpets, even though the product generates many negative impacts on the environment, being oil-derived (through nylon polymers), chemicals-based (glues) to name but a few detrimental aspects. The point was to be able one day to make fully sustainable carpets. This is a key point to remember: unlike some pioneers in the field, the company did not have sustainability in its DNA. This raises the question of whether any industrial activity may be legitimate in becoming sustainable. Which leads us back to CSR: for Anderson, making carpets could become a socially responsible business activity. Could the same apply to legal but controversial products such as tobacco or weapons? As we will see, even though carpets are not so controversial, embedding sustainability did raise the issue of the product's intrinsic social and environmental benefits.

The journey thus began in 1995. The first major step for Interface was to partner with some of the world's cutting-edge environmental experts from the time, such as the Swedish NGO The Natural Step, biomimicry's founder Jannine Benyus and Paul Hawken himself (to name but a few), what Ray Anderson described as his "dream team". This is the cornerstone of the whole process: working with the right experts and partners to deploy the sustainability strategy was clearly the main driver.

---

[22] See Ray Anderson's interview in *The Corporation*, a documentary released in 2003. See also his book *Confessions of a Radical Industrialist: How Interface proved that you can build a successful business without destroying the planet* (2011).

Another key element was the need for intense stakeholder consultation: Ray Anderson spent several months talking to his most critical stakeholders, namely the shareholders and the employees to convince them of the relevance of his initiative. According to Anderson, this was an "absolute necessity".[23] Regarding shareholders, it was almost a matter of survival since the stock price had plummeted after the company's public announcement that it was about to radically change the way its products were made to become sustainable... and this was all the harder to grasp back in 1995!

Following a systemic approach inspired by the school of natural capitalism and biomimicry, Interface developed its "seven fronts" strategy, an integral approach which addressed concurrently seven priorities: elimination of waste, benign emissions, renewable energy, closing the loop, resource efficient transportation, sensitization of stakeholders, and redesigning of commerce. Needless to say that such an approach was revolutionary at the time, one of the very first industrial applications of nature-based economic models. What was also quite unique was to address all the fronts simultaneously, whereas most companies tend to adopt a step-by-step approach.

After having elaborated its sustainable model and strategy, the company then started to operationalize it by setting up appropriate metrics (in 1996) and using innovative tools such as Life Cycle Analyses to evaluate the environmental impact of its products during their entire lifetime. Thus, from the start, sustainability was embedded in the value chain, from R&D to manufacturing and to product use and disposal. Targets were then set for each of the seven fronts. A few years later, this strategy was enveloped in a unique ambition, "Mission Zero" which aimed at having no negative impact on the environment by 2020!

One of the key findings of the life cycle analysis was that 63% of the carpet tile's impact on the environment actually occurred before the manufacturing stage, due to the raw materials employed. This prompted Interface to take another quite innovative step, namely attempting to bring its suppliers "on board" with their new strategy since without them the objectives could never be reached. Although this proved hard to do, one

---

[23] Private conversation with the author.

of Interface's key suppliers, Italian yarn manufacturer Aquafil, agreed to cooperate. They aimed to drastically reduce the negative environmental impacts of yarn: the main objective then became recycling nylon, at a time when everybody maintained that it was impossible.

In retrospect, we can say that the journey towards sustainability at Interface was launched successfully thanks to the convergence of multiple factors:

- An inspirational leader with a cutting-edge vision who set the course.
- A corporate culture and values conducive to change and innovation since Interface was already known in the industry as a highly innovative company, a company which is also constantly looking forward ("there is always a solution") and able to learn from its mistakes ("successful failures").
- A company that has always favored a horizontal entrepreneurial culture, with everybody's ideas and suggestions are heard and possibly implemented.
- A clearly integrated vision, embedded in the daily operations.
- The engagement of all employees and of critical stakeholders such as investors and suppliers.
- And last but not least, a constant search for performance and value creation. Indeed, the company never lost sight of its business priority: the journey towards sustainability constantly sought value creation through design, marketing and product performance. Sustainability was not meant to be yet another marketing campaign, but rather the foundation supporting product development and marketing.

2.2 *Interface today*

Today, even though Interface has not reached its zero impact objective yet,[24] the company can boast very impressive results regarding resource use and impact mitigation: from its 1996 baseline, the company has cut its greenhouse gas emissions by 96%, its water intake by 88% (its Dutch factory uses no water), its overall energy use by 43% and its product carbon

---

[24] The company reckons that they have reached about 70% of the target.

footprint by 66%. The percentage of renewable energy has reached 86% overall, with 100% in the Netherlands!

One of the key success factors is undoubtedly Interface's constant drive toward sustainability through innovation and design. In this respect, the huge savings made from resource cuts enabled the company to finance its sustainability objectives. On the other hand, sustainability itself was from the start of the journey closely associated with product development and marketing. To take a few examples, random design carpets were an imitation of autumn forest floors giving them a very innovative design while at the same time making it easy to replace a part without changing the whole pattern. To replace the glue used for the underlayer, Interface invented "tactiles", square stickers made from recycled material. This enabled easier installation and removal of the carpet tiles while drastically reducing the negative environmental impact. Lastly, reducing the environmental footprint pushed the company to produce thinner carpets, which in turn allowed it to enter Southern European markets where hard floors are far more popular.

Nevertheless, Interface did encounter several failures: for instance, the product to service shift did not work at first, since clients were not ready to lease carpets instead of buying them. In other words, the market was not ready. But today, the program has been relaunched and has been much more successful. Another striking case is that of a program launched in 2008 called FairWorks by which Interface started developing luxury carpet floors inspired from traditional designs in cooperation with local Indian NGOs. This was a way for the company to add a strong social pillar to its environmental sustainability policy. The program turned out to be a complete failure, clients not being ready to buy more than just a yard to hang on their walls for decoration! But Interface learned from this and launched Net-Works a few years later as we will see below. This is what may be called a business case for successful failures!

More generally speaking, Interface is constantly striving to close the loop on its products: recycled and biobased materials have increased by 58%, its supplier Aquafil did manage to recycle nylon and eventually started selling it to Interface but also to its competitors... Faced with this loss of a competitive sustainability-related advantage, Interface investigated new potential sources of sustainably sourced raw materials and came up with an innovative inclusive and circular business called Net-Works. The program is centered around the collection of discarded nylon fishing nets which are found around the world and cause damage to the marine environment, polluting coastal ecosystems and beaches, causing the death of fish thus negatively affecting local fishing communities.

Interface launched Net-Works in 2012 in partnership with the highly reputable conservation society Zoological Society of London (ZSL), its supplier Aquafil as well as local NGOs based in the Philippines where the program was first launched. Net-Works is a unique inclusive and circular business model deeply rooted in a triple bottom line approach: the benefits are *social*, since the fishing nets are collected by poor local communities who benefit from additional income and are encouraged to pool their savings in local community banks, *environmental*, thanks to the cleaning of beaches and coastal waters, and *economic*, since the fishing nets are reprocessed and then re-enter the production loop.

Net-Works is an innovative model which is beneficial to both Interface and Aquafil as well as to impoverished communities. It further shows that a circular approach may also generate positive social impacts. For Interface, this is a way of strengthening the social dimension of its sustainability journey. Besides, the company is fully aware of the two key challenges the program faces: the need to scale up to increase the impact and the obligation to think long-term since collecting fishing nets is a temporary solution for generating additional community income. Thus, after having been tested for several years in the Philippines, Net-Works is now being implemented in Cameroon. Regarding the long-term prospects, Interface is working with local partners to provide new sources of income to local populations once there are no more fishing nets to collect. This also means that awareness campaigns have been launched to prevent fishing nets from being thrown away. Instead, local fishermen can sell them back to Interface and Aquafil directly.

Today, despite the fact that Ray Anderson passed away in 2011, the Interface model is stronger than ever. The company is involved in several projects with the U.N., strongly supporting the Sustainable Development Goals; it is also lobbying for stricter regulation on product environmental declarations in the E.U. Interface has remained the leader in its market all these years, and it is interesting to point out that sustainability up until recently was not their main sales argument. The point was not to market supposedly "green" carpets but to offer the best products in terms of quality and design, and to produce them sustainably.

With the 2020 deadline approaching, the company keeps looking ahead and beyond. Using a "backcasting" approach (what would we like the world and Interface to be like in the future and what can we do to make it happen?), Interface launched a few years ago its new 2030 strategy, *Climate Take Back.*

2.3 *Interface tomorrow?*

"Climate take back" is a very ambitious strategy: whereas it was once restorative, the company now aims at being "regenerative", i.e. having a net positive impact on climate, which means for instance no longer seeing carbon as a threat, but rather as a resource, eventually reversing climate change. Actually, Interface is already producing a carpet tile called "Proof Positive" which is carbon negative! It has also introduced the concept of "factories as forests", meaning that a factory should aim at producing the same ecological benefits as a forest ecosystem. This seems purely utopian, but the company is working with innovative start-ups and researchers to work toward creating an ecosystem within the factory which is modelled after a forest ecosystem.

In addition to factories as forests, Interface see tomorrow as the time when the industrial re-revolution will take place, with full circularity, carbon sequestering products, products made from dispersed materials and a supply chain that benefits all life… While constantly boosting innovation, this strategy is for Interface the most appropriate way to be resilient in the future.

This may seem totally unrealistic, yet Interface has started to cooperate with other businesses to reach this aim, identifying disruptive start-ups which may eventually provide the right solutions. The key word here is cooperation: cooperation within the industry, and cooperation with civil society, as well as international, regional and national institutions.

Of course, challenges abound: will the company be able to maintain its objectives while accelerating its growth? How about stock market threats? Will the new products meet clients' demands? In any case, this is a unique model, and one may wonder why it has not been replicated across industry. Some of the reasons might include the extraordinary convergence of multiple positive factors, and also the fact that this is a B2B company operating within a fairly narrow range of products. One can easily imagine how much harder it must be for multinationals with dozens of different product lines and which have an imperious need to communicate to the general public. This definitely makes all the difference.

Interface is clearly paving the way for a *paradigm shift* whereby industry fully reinvents itself by learning from nature: how it produces, how it designs things, how it recycles... Can one still speak of CSR? Interface is indeed a socially responsible company, in the strongest sense of the word, even though it nevers uses the term. However, sustainability is so embedded in the overall business strategy that traditional CSR seems far removed...

This is the final lesson one can draw from the Interface journey: if CSR is to be fully embedded to be tangible and efficient, it seems that sustainability would appear to be the only answer. This leads us to wonder whether we should not stop using the term CSR which is ultimately misleading and confusing.

Why not clearly distinguish between sustainability-driven responsibility on the one hand, and philanthropy on the other? It seems that in a few years from now compliance-based CSR will have become so commonplace that companies all over the world will be facing a crossroads: either they embark on the sustainability journey, always keeping in mind the triple bottom line, or they will naturally go back to the "give back" approach, although probably in a rebranded way, but the core intention will remain the same.

As we have seen in this chapter, there is much to learn from nature, and this particularly applies to the manufacturing world. Many could object to the fact that this is not very relevant for services. But the answer is clear: sustainability means preserving nature of course, but it also means caring about people and the economy. If we want to sustain life on our planet, those three dimensions are totally interrelated. And business can do much to make it possible!

CHAPTER 6

TOMORROW'S CSR AGENDA

CSR has become a buzzword around the world. From Peru to China, from Vietnam to Russia, from Kenya to the Emirates, more and more local companies are developing CSR actions and policies, local NGOs and grassroots organizations are created to promote CSR and business schools are integrating it in their curricula.

Yet, skepticism and criticism often prevail when it comes to the real impact of CSR policies. One of the main causes is undoubtedly the fact that today's CSR has become an umbrella term which covers very diverse approaches which result in from mere Public Relations gimmicks to strategic embeddedness. This is certainly due to the fact that the CSR concept is constantly evolving, due to how it has spread across extremely diverse cultural and institutional environments. Moreover, the roles of key stakeholders such as government and consumers vary greatly from one country to another.

This final chapter attempts to forecast how CSR will evolve in the coming decade or so. To do so, we shall focus on some key issues and trends which we believe will likely have a decisive influence in the near future. Our hypotheses are based on one main assumption, namely the fact that the term "CSR" could disappear in the coming years or at least branch out into several distinct approaches.

Another important point to be taken into account is the fact that CSR has only just started to spread across the developing world and it remains difficult to foresee the form it will take in the coming years. However, we shall endeavor to propose some personal reflections nourished by our experience in several developing countries in different parts of the world.

Finally, we shall look at the broader picture, namely our role as consumers and citizens in a world where social and environmental challenges are more and more pressing, and where social inequalities are growing every day, both locally and globally.

1. Is the end of CSR near?

It seems quite paradoxical to raise such a question at a time when the term itself has never been so widely used. Yet, as we have shown in the previous chapters of this book, CSR covers so many different types of actions and policies that no unified definition exists. If we look back, CSR was born in a very specific cultural and business context, that of the U.S. where it developed mostly as a philanthropic-contractualist instrument for companies ethically required to give back to society. Several decades later, CSR arrived in continental Europe where it took another turn, especially under the influence of the newly born concept of sustainability. And yet the European Union chose the concept of CSR to describe the sustainability challenge for businesses. Later, CSR started to spread all over the world, through the globalization of value chains and new social and environmental requirements from multinationals. What appears as a "hybridization" process is reflected in the terminology used by companies today, from corporate citizenship, values, commitments and engagement to CSR and sustainability.

This leads us to distinguish between two dominant forms of CSR today:

1) Philanthropy which is a universal practice and is currently undergoing major changes, especially in the developed world, where it is turning into a strategic process, aimed at creating value for both the company and for the communities whose interests it is serving.
2) Sustainability-driven policies aimed at embedding some key social and/or environmental priorities into the overall strategy and operations. This requires a comprehensive materiality review of CSR issues as well as appropriate management and reporting tools.

In both cases, compliance-based social and environmental policies and tools are increasingly playing a part. Indeed, institutional, market as well as societal pressures are prompting companies around the world to adopt international soft law instruments to show their willingness to comply with generally accepted international standards, which means anything from superficial engagements to strict compliance processes. The prevailing trend today among businesses seems to be a soft and reactive compliance approach aimed at minimizing the most negative impacts of their activity and operations on critical stakeholders, be they the government, customers, employees, suppliers or society at large.

1.1. *Social responsibility or corporate sustainability?*

Consequently, it has become irrelevant to use the same term, CSR, to describe practices which differ so much in nature and impact. "CSR" has thus become a misleading concept, especially if one thinks of the meaning of "responsibility" in either case. Responsibility in the case of philanthropy boils down to the company donating money to help the community on moral/ethical grounds. Even though philanthropy is becoming more investment-oriented, the bottom line remains the willingness to do good (mostly) through financial assistance. In the case of shared value approaches, the willingness to do good to the community is meant primarily to serve the business interests of the company at the same time.

Given the often-pejorative connotation of philanthropy, why not call it "social responsibility" with reference to its very roots? In addition, the C for corporate seems to be less meaningful since philanthropy is an inside-out process: as previously stated, the biggest philanthropists may well be the worst corporate actors when it comes to their internal environmental and social responsibilities. Given that most philanthropy-driven approaches integrate some degree of compliance-based policies, the point is not so much to extend the company's "social responsibility" but rather the obligation to be compliant with internationally recognized practices regarding social and environmental issues. Of course, this process partially engages the company's responsibility, but this responsibility either prods the company toward quasi-legal obligations and thus is less voluntary or it remains non-binding as is most of the soft law governing CSR today.

As for the second and more recent type of "CSR", we suggest that it be called *corporate sustainability* since the main aim is to embed social, environmental and ethical issues into the overall strategy and vision of the company, thus pursuing both a business-related and stakeholder-based long-term commitment. In this case, the concept of responsibility takes on a much deeper and broader meaning, such as defined by German philosopher Hans Jonas: being responsible by acting now so as to make the future possible and sustainable.[1]

This raises a fundamental issue as to the role of business in society: if we adhere to the "CSR-as-usual" form, businesses contribute to society by sharing some of their profits, they are responsible insofar as they are willing to give back to society. To put it differently, the company recognizes that stakeholders other than the shareholders are entitled to a share of the success. In the case of corporate sustainability, the company directly contributes to responding to the sustainability challenges; it is in itself a provider of common goods and turns *de facto* into a political actor.

Our conviction is that businesses today are bound to do their share when it comes to providing responses to the huge social and environmental challenges facing our planet. Businesses can only do so by transforming themselves radically, which entails redefining their purpose, their mission, redesigning their products and services so that they become part of the solution. Of course, this may work only if this radical transformation provides businesses with new sources of innovation and business opportunities. At the end of the day, business will never contribute positively to society if, in doing so, they do not generate enough profits!

Some may argue that strategic philanthropy is another way of meeting this objective; in our opinion, however, philanthropy may be considered as a support scheme, but not as the core justification of the company's social responsibility. The main asset of corporate philanthropy seems to be its non-profit dimension which enables companies to free themselves from the profitability imperative and engage in certain actions they would never be able to undertake if they had to comply with profit-related rules.

---

[1] See Introduction.

1.2. The case for corporate sustainability

Given the magnitude of certain social and environmental issues on our planet today, it is only by embedding sustainability at the core that businesses will genuinely fulfill their responsibilities and generate a tangible positive long-term impact through their products, services and operations.

Fortunately enough, more and more CEOs are convinced that having such a purpose in business is essential today. Yet, obstacles abound: first and foremost, it remains difficult to put sustainability at the core of the business due to the market and its short-term pressures. Indeed, all the financial ratios and indicators currently in use clearly favor short-termism. The financial world obsessively awaits the quarterly results, and most shareholders continue to think short-term when it comes to their dividends. Engaging in a sustainability-driven transformation still means running against the tide!

1.2.1. Legal and governance issues

Indeed, one crucial point that remains is that of the shareholders' attitude towards sustainability. Although sustainability is still viewed by many as a waste of time and money and an undue burden, several positive evolutions must be stressed. First, some of the most influential investors today are undeniably showing an increasing interest in sustainability-related issues.

To take the most striking case, the asset-management firm Blackrock, a major global player in corporate investment, made the news in January 2018 when its boss Larry Fink published a letter to all CEOs entitled "A Sense of Purpose" in which he passionately implored investors to change their way of thinking with regard to what business is meant to accomplish: His key point was that the private sector must listen to the demands of society and integrate them into their strategies:

> "*As a result, society increasingly is turning to the private sector and asking that companies respond to broader societal challenges. Indeed, the public expectations of your company have never been greater.*

Society is demanding that companies, both public and private, serve a social purpose. To prosper over time, every company must not only deliver financial performance, but also show how it makes a positive contribution to society. Companies must benefit all of their stakeholders, including shareholders, employees, customers, and the communities in which they operate.[2]

Fink went even further by stating that taking stakeholders' demands into account was not only a response to societal pressures but also a necessity for achieving full business potential:

"Without a sense of purpose, no company, either public or private, can achieve its full potential. It will ultimately lose the license to operate from key stakeholders. It will succumb to short-term pressures to distribute earnings, and, in the process, sacrifice investments in employee development, innovation, and capital expenditures that are necessary for long-term growth. It will remain exposed to activist campaigns that articulate a clearer goal, even if that goal serves only the shortest and narrowest of objectives. And ultimately, that company will provide sub-par returns to the investors who depend on it to finance their retirement, home purchases, or higher education."

Some will argue that this is a mere PR exercise. Be that as it may, it is a strong signal that the case for corporate sustainability is increasingly being acknowledged among the most influential financial actors. Sustainability is starting to be seen as a pre-requisite for long-term thinking and renewed license to operate.

Regarding shareholders in general, major institutional investors like U.S. pension funds are increasingly pushing companies to focus on social and environmental issues. Such is the case of CALPERS urging oil and gas majors to do much more to act against climate change.

Yet, the dominant governance structures are still rather timid about sustainability. Corporate Boards hardly consider sustainability-related issues as priority topics. This largely depends of course on Board

---

[2] Larry Fink's *Annual Letter to CEOs: A Sense of Purpose* (January, 2018), retrieved online at https://www.blackrock.com/corporate/investor-relations/larry-fink-ceo-letter

compositions, such as the presence or not of independent non-executive members. As for shareholders' annual meetings, they still leave little or no room at all for sustainability and CSR. While audit committees are quite common, ethics and CSR committees remain rare.

In short, dominant governance patterns still reflect a purely financial view of the companies; it is urgent that the latter undergo major transformations so that stakeholders' views are fully taken into account with regard to key strategic decisions. Seen from a CSR perspective, shareholders need to be considered as full-fledged stakeholders which supposes having them on board when it comes to sustainability-driven transformation. The founder of Interface Ray Anderson confessed to me that it took him about two years to convince the company's shareholders of the benefits of embarking on their sustainability journey.

Another major potential evolution is related to the evolution of the law itself on the role and purpose of companies. As we saw in Chapter 2, some countries have started creating new legal forms of business in which their social and environmental aims are on par with their profit objective. This is the case of community interest companies in Great Britain and B-Corporations in a large number of States in the U.S. These hybrid forms clearly facilitate the pursuit of impact-driven policies while meeting the expectations of purpose-driven investors. Attempts like those in France to broaden the legal definition of a company are other promising trends.

Regarding soft law, the growing popularity of the B-Corp certification is another tangible positive trend. This private certification scheme issued by global non-profit organization B-Lab requires for-profit companies to reach and maintain a minimum score based on their social and environmental performance. Today there are over 2,600 certified B Corporations across 150 industries in over 50 countries. Some multinationals are even aiming to obtain it, such as the French company Danone. Indeed, it has already managed to obtain B-Corp certification for five of its subsidiaries and is hoping to get it for all of its operations in the future.

The main advantage of this certification is its global outreach: indeed, companies from all over the world including developing countries are striving to obtain it. This definitely gives momentum to "business with a purpose" views. The rather flexible and non-binding nature of the scheme makes it an accessible instrument. Of course, some will argue against this type of certification since the very nature of it may lead to a lack of guarantee due to a fairly loose control of the performance of the certified companies. Yet it is clearly pushing the sustainability agenda across the globe.

1.2.2. *The case of family businesses*

CSR literature has long overlooked family businesses since they are usually small or medium-sized and are not listed on stock markets. Yet, they represent an overwhelming proportion of businesses at the global scale, especially in the developing world. Several surveys also point out the growing percentage of family businesses among large enterprises. At the global scale, it is expected that 40% of large enterprises will be family businesses by 2025.[3] In Asia, the latter already represent about 80% to 90% of all large enterprises.

While there is a plethora of management literature on the competitive advantages of family businesses such as their resilience, organizational flexibility and values-oriented corporate culture, little has been said about the great potential advantage they may have to offer when it comes to embedding sustainability in their policies.

Indeed, family businesses are naturally inclined to look to the future, the question of succession being crucial for them. Intergenerational transmission goes hand in hand with a keen sense of the long-term. Furthermore, families are more likely to express common values that they are keen on sharing with their employees. These values may be further reinforced by the need to remain united in the face of potential external acquirers.

Thus, from a perspective of time and ethics, family businesses are much better "equipped" to embed sustainability in their vision. As previously mentioned in this book, the fact that the Mars company has engaged in a long-term program with cocoa farmers in the Côte d'Ivoire is largely due to the fact that the company is entirely controlled by the family. Indeed, it would certainly be interesting to study the positive correlation between companies engaged in corporate sustainability strategies and their family business structure.

---

[3] McKinsey report, 2014.

Yet, most family businesses around the world tend to have a traditional paternalistic approach, or, in other words, a philanthropic view of their responsibility to society. This is especially the case in Asia where some families have been running the same companies for generations. A prime example is the world-renowned Indian company Tata owned by the family holding Tata Sons.

Nevertheless, we trust that shifting to corporate sustainability for family companies is more than plausible in the future as long as social and environmental issues are embedded in the family values. In other words, the move toward sustainability-driven values is most likely to come from family businesses especially in the developing world. Besides, the next generation is likely to be much more naturally inclined to believe that such issues are top priorities.

1.3. Some assumptions about the evolution of CSR in developing countries

As we saw previously, CSR in the developing world is largely characterized by traditional philanthropy and a gradual move to soft compliance approaches. This move toward compliance is certainly due to the emergence of global value chains: local companies on the one hand are increasingly being pressured by their international clients to adopt compliance-related CSR tools such as standards and certifications and more broadly speaking to comply with their CSR policies. On the other hand, local subsidiaries of Western multinationals also contribute to diffusing CSR locally since they are obliged by the Head Office to report on their social and environmental performance.

At the same time, the local social and environmental regulatory requirements in most developing countries are quite low: thus, the pressure will not come from government and regulators. Similarly, local consumers still have little awareness of sustainability issues or perhaps they simply have other urgent priorities.

In such a context, local family businesses which account for the vast majority of all businesses rely on traditional philanthropic practices usually associated with religious habits. Such is the case, for example, in Latin America, India and the Middle East where local companies finance local health care services, schools and sports facilities and it is not uncommon for them to offer scholarships to their employee's children. Even though more and more of these local companies have adopted a CSR approach, the level of compliance-based CSR remains low given the minimal amount of institutional pressure. Furthermore, corruption and the lack of democratic control are often additional aggravating factors.

Given the overall situation, what might spur developing country companies to move toward adopting corporate sustainability approaches?

First, the growing presence of the 17 Sustainable Development Goals (SDGs) appears to be a positive sign: the local Global Compact networks set up by the U.N. clearly contribute to diffusing new approaches and practices locally. Given the fact that the Global Compact and its 10 principles are now supplemented by the 17 SDGs, local networks urge companies to take the lead and actively commit to embedding sustainability in their strategies. In many countries, several local companies have been chosen to be the leaders on specific SDGs. Hopefully this still-recent movement will prove effective in the medium-term.

If one may thus expect a gradual integration of compliance-based sustainability policies in the developing world, our assumption is that a key priority for most companies will be the social aspect of sustainability. Based on observations and studies from different parts of the word, it is clear that the number one priority for a large majority of companies is the workforce and their surrounding communities.

Indeed, companies need to move away from traditional human resource practices generating many negative side effects. Local businesses certainly have a major responsibility to treat people fairly and decently and provide them with improved working conditions, and more generally speaking opportunities for long-term personal development. This also implies engaging employees in meaningful projects to inspire them and boost their motivation, and thus their productivity.

To take a few concrete examples, these projects can take the form of providing female employees in South East Asian textile factories with better protection against domestic violence often arising from a nonexistent work-life balance due to excessive overtime. In many state-owned companies and in services industries such as banks, CSR can play a decisive role in boosting employee commitment.

Faced with the failure of local governments to ensure a decent quality of life in so many developing countries, the local business community truly appears to be the sole change-maker. But in order to provide tangible long-term positive impacts, companies need to distance themselves from traditional assistance and adopt a sustainability-driven approach to social issues. In this respect, some socially focused SDGs may prove to be relevant tools for companies wishing to embed these priorities into their strategy and their operations.

This move to corporate sustainability depends of course on top management's ability to understand the benefits the company can gain from this in the longer term. For instance, by empowering their employees or by boosting their actual impact on local economic development and focusing on excluded populations, such businesses create long-term value and new business opportunities such as international expansion and innovation-driven product and service developments.

This is just the beginning of the journey, but one can expect that CSR in the developing world will give way to a new innovative hybrid form of CSR which is strongly oriented toward sustainability-driven social engagement. As for the environmental side, one can expect the new generation of managers and employees to become increasingly aware of what is at stake and exert pressure on company CEOs and political leaders to put CSR at the top of their priority list. Indeed, the Generations Y (the Millennials) and Z will no doubt be key drivers in mainstreaming sustainability and embedding it into the political, social and economic agendas of businesses around the world. Today, all surveys show just how important environmental sustainability is for these generations... And this is not only the case in developed countries!

1.4. *CSR as a catalyst for social innovation*

Embedding sustainability-driven CSR into their strategy is a major challenge for companies since it inevitably raises the issue of the relevance of their business model. More and more companies are currently wondering about how they can transform their business models so as to integrate key social and environmental issues, yet several obstacles stand in the way.

Indeed, what is at stake for a company is its capacity to innovate without losing sight of its financial objectives. The sustainability-driven innovation process requires a disruptive mindset given the radical changes needed. A company might decide to dedicate a substantial portion of its R&D budget to sustainability-driven innovations. Yet, this may not be financially feasible or even incompatible with the current R&D approach or mindset of the company.

Some companies may create specific internal units dedicated to innovative product developments or business models. This is the case of pharmaceutical company Sanofi which created an "Access to Medicines" division in order to provide appropriate medicines for the poor populations in least developed countries. In order for it to achieve its goal, this division is not subjected to the usual profitability requirements. For Sanofi, this endeavor is both a way of exercising its social responsibility while investing in the future as it will be a great source of inspiration.

Another means to innovate is to set up a specific investment fund dedicated to sustainable innovation. One of the pioneers in this field was French multinational Danone which, in 2006, created the Danone Communities Fund,[4] the purpose of which is to finance social businesses which do not have any profitability requirements. Yet, these social businesses are real businesses since they are expected to make profits, but the latter are to be entirely reinvested in the project. For its first project in Bangladesh, Danone partnered with modern microcredit inventor and Nobel Peace Prize Winner, Muhammad Yunus.

The founder of microfinance institution Grameen Bank, Yunus strongly believes in the need to partner with multinationals to create social businesses, the aim of which is to solve urgent social and environmental issues. The rule for these businesses is to put impact before profit. The first joint venture was thus between Grameen Bank and Danone to produce a highly nutritional yoghurt for the poor called *Shoktidoi*. The first factory was built in 2006 near the town of Bogra and began producing yoghurt with local employees and suppliers. The distribution system was organized around Grameen ladies[5] selling the yoghurt door-to-door in the Bogra region.

---

[4] A socially responsible investment fund 10% of which is dedicated to "pure" social businesses, i.e. that do not generate any returns for investors.

[5] The Grameen ladies are women hired by the Grameen bank to collect the microloans.

The objective of the project was to create a yoghurt that would provide children with 30% of their daily nutritional needs but would be sold at an affordable price for poor populations (6 cents of a euro). The project required major R&D investments from Danone, partnerships with international and local NGOs and public actors (the local hospital). Strongly built on a triple bottom line approach (green facilities, eco-friendly packaging, microloans for the local farmers, supplementary income for the Grameen ladies, impact measurement on health, etc.), this was clearly an impressive project from a social innovation perspective. Unfortunately, the 2008 financial crisis and the distribution model had a severe negative impact on the sales objectives. Today, the project has been relaunched with a mainstream distribution model to complement the original model.

Danone certainly learned a lot from this social business experiment. Even though the proposed business plan seemed utterly unrealistic, the project required great innovation which gave Danone new insights into high impact nutritional products, relations with local stakeholders in poor countries, and multi-stakeholder initiatives. This case is a typical example of reverse innovation, i.e. the fact that frugal innovation designed for Bottom of Pyramid markets may result in findings that can be applied to other more mature markets. From a business perspective, this helped the multinational better understand Bottom of Pyramid markets and adapt more quickly to non-mature markets. Let us also not underestimate the fact that this CSR-driven project was also an opportunity for Danone to get a foothold in a potentially lucrative market, a country of 150 million inhabitants with a rising middle class.

Following this semi-failure, Danone decided to no longer set up any innovative social businesses, but rather invest in new promising social and environmental ventures. For example, the company acquired a stake in other Danone Communities Fund projects related to water and milk supply. Internally, Danone has also set up two endowment funds: the Danone Ecosystem and Livelihoods Funds. These help the company reach its sustainability objectives by enabling it to test new business models such as the empowerment of local farming communities and the co-creation of inclusive business solutions.

The Danone case demonstrates how embedding CSR strategically can lead to the launch of social innovation experiments with non profit-driven funds, thus making it possible to test new models without having a sword of Damocles — profit margins — hanging over them...

An increasing number of companies, especially in Europe, are currently engaging in similar initiatives, such as setting up their own impact investment funds to acquire stakes in innovative social and environmental startups, possibly acquiring such startups... In other words, building up competence in alternative sustainability-driven business models.

A key lesson to be drawn from this trend is how urgent it has become for committed businesses to externalize their learning processes and partner with social entrepreneurs, NGOs, grassroots organizations, and local governments. Corporate Foundations are also becoming more strategic by financing social entrepreneurs instead of donating to NGOs. Sustainability is in fact blurring the lines between businesses and other actors. Cooperation is the key to success.

At the end of the day, the initial CSR strategy appears to be the main catalyst for social innovation and transformational change. Even though this evolution remains limited in numbers, we can bet on the fact that such multi-stakeholder social innovation initiatives are likely to boom and spread around the world in the coming years. This is indeed the only way of finding the right answers to today's highly intricate sustainability challenges.

1.5. The need for accountability: Recent trends in reporting

The fact that CSR has changed so radically means that companies must now be fully accountable to multiple stakeholders for their initiatives and policies. Indeed, stakeholders expect businesses to communicate on their sustainability-related performance. This explains why reporting has become a fundamental dimension of CSR today. Gone are the days when companies could simply issue glossy brochures with beautiful pictures they called CSR or Corporate Citizenship reports. Stakeholders, from governments to consumers to civil society organizations are now asking for facts, nothing but the facts...

At the international level, the Global Reporting Initiative (GRI) has definitely played an important role in advocating the standardization of sustainability reporting. Today more and more companies are complying with the whole GRI framework, i.e. its general principles and its 80 or so indicators. The much-needed third-party validation is gradually gaining ground, even though it is still rarely required by national authorities. The "comply or explain" principle is also becoming commonplace, meaning that companies may have to be more forthcoming about some hidden aspects of their CSR policies.

The European Union is clearly showing the way: its 2014 Directive on non-financial reporting[6] has made it compulsory for the approximately 6,000 large "public-interest" companies[7] to disclose information about their social and environmental management and performance (including Board diversity). From 2018 onward, companies will have to include non-financial statements in their annual reports. The Directive also requires that statutory auditors validate the existence of a non-financial statement. Several member States have gone even further by requiring third-party assurance statements (i.e. validating the data).

Outside the E.U., non-financial reporting practices are now becoming common around the world. Yet, comparability and industry benchmarks remain limited because of the lack of harmonization of practices and the still rare third-party validations. Reporting remains all too often performative rather than informative. Numbers are usually displayed in absolute values which means little to the reader. The historical nature of the data and precise future targets are sometimes lacking. This is largely due to the separate CSR report "exercise": companies tend to be over-influenced by their external communications departments which are prone to overplaying the company's CSR achievements. Ultimately, many reports are hybrid documents, a cross between genuine non-financial reports and didactic communication brochures about the company's CSR initiatives.

One promising development is that of integrated reporting[8] which has developed over the last few years. The objective is to provide a single view of corporate performance by aggregating key financial and non-financial

---

[6] Directive 2014/95/EU.

[7] Due to the national transposition process, some E.U. member States may include specific types of businesses, such as state-owned or privately controlled companies with more than 500 employees.

[8] Promoted by the IIRC, http://integratedreporting.org/

data. Integrated reporting is intended to reflect the strategic embeddedness of sustainability. This is a very innovative approach to reporting which requires a real shift in mindset and organizational practices from the companies. Companies need to have a sufficient maturity level to combine CSR and finance in a single document that reflects the overall strategy of the company. Even though current integrated reports often remain somewhat imperfect, companies are learning fast and are moving toward disruptive approaches such as measuring value creation per stakeholder and proving to shareholders that sustainability-driven performance is beneficial to them.

It can be expected that the majority of companies engaged in sustainability will move toward integrated reporting in the near future. According to the latest estimates, around 2,000 companies published integrated reports in 2017.[9] Interestingly enough, the practice is spreading across the world, from the European Union to the U.S. to Japan. Eventually reporting for both shareholders and other stakeholders will become the common standard. At that point, social responsibility will have become an integral part of business.

However, there is still a long way to go before social responsibility becomes the norm. The companies engaging in sustainability embeddedness are still few and far between. Moreover, most of them are struggling to impose their vision on their often-reluctant shareholders. Shareholders want regular and substantial yields on their investments, especially pension funds which represent millions of U.S. retirees. Climbing Mount Sustainability, as Interface CEO Ray Anderson used to say, requires relentless determination and long-term resilience.

All things considered, the key driving force is in our hands — we, the consumers-citizens, can play a decisive role in pushing sustainability further.

2. Ultimately, it's our call

It is far from easy to imagine how CSR will evolve in the coming decade: one can assume that an increasing number of companies around the world will adopt mimetic approaches and converge toward some common

---

[9] IIRC source.

compliance-based forms of CSR. From a regulatory standpoint, it remains hard to tell how much more stringent legislation will become with regard to social responsibility and the environment. Most experts believed that regulation would inevitably lose ground in the face of globalization and open markets, yet recent trends clearly indicate a relative return to regulatory approaches.[10]

Will CSR shift massively towards corporate sustainability strategies or will it remain predominantly philanthropy-driven? The answer clearly depends on the pressure exerted by consumers. Indeed, our consumption choices will have a decisive impact on companies's transformation processes. By and large, if consumers do not radically change their habits and demands, philanthropy will most certainly remain a predominant form of CSR, all the more so as there is an increasing disengagement of governments in the field of social policies in most developed countries.

In other words, we consumers are the main driving force capable of inciting a growing number of companies to move toward embedding CSR in their core strategies and operations. Indeed, business model transformation will accelerate only if the demand for profound change is strong enough.

However, several emerging trends lead us to opt for the business transformation scenario. First, a growing number of consumers in the developed world are challenging the dominant post World War II consumer society model. Surveys carried out in Europe and North America over the last decade indicate that an ever-increasing number of consumers wish to behave in a responsible way, i.e. they tend to favor the social, environmental and health-related benefits of products, which increasingly leads them to adopt new purchasing habits. The most telling illustration of this is the incredible boom in organic products over the last decade.

Western consumers now more often seek out healthy and ethical products. In France for instance, the latest surveys indicate that 65% of the consumers take into account the true social and environmental benefits of a product when shopping.[11] Of course, this does not mean that these consumers will only buy such products. Due to conflicting impulses consumers' shopping habits remain quite contradictory and paradoxical. Yet, the

---

[10] See Chapter 4 on hard law approaches to human rights.
[11] Greenflex Responsible consumption surveys available at https://www.greenflex.com/en/

sustainability dimension has definitely become a key variable in the act of purchasing.

As a consequence, labels have become very fashionable: more and more companies are adopting environmental, social and ethical certification to meet consumers' expectations. However, this may well just be a transitory phase. Indeed, faced with the proliferation of labels of all kinds, from the most reliable third-party certified, to the 100% self-declared type, consumers are becoming increasingly wary and demanding that companies do more. Full product transparency and accountability are the newest trends: a significant number of consumers expect brands to give all possible guarantees on the origin of the product and the relative social and environmental benefits. In other words, "walking the talk" and "just the facts" seem to be the new mantras for a growing number of consumers in the Western world.

Of course, this trend toward socially responsible consumption is limited by economic factors: on average, such products remain overpriced and ill-suited to the purchasing power of medium and lower income citizens. Yet, the latter are increasingly prepared to buy less but better quality, and thereby include sustainability-related criteria in their choices. The "less is more" movement is not a fad, we believe that this gradual rejection of over-consumption and hypermaterialism is a real sign of a long-term change.

The "buying local" trend may represent a compromise between price constraints and responsible shopping behavior. Western consumers feel the need to reconnect to their territory and their culture; they increasingly distrust industrially processed food and the recurring sanitary scandals in this industry. From the locavores in the U.S. to the slow food movement in Italy, consumers in developed countries are increasingly seeking natural, healthy food produced ethically and locally.

Regarding household appliances, the unsustainable "programmed obsolescence" strategy is prompting more and more buyers to choose premium products with a longer life span. In the field of cosmetics, chemical substances are being banned more and more frequently. With regard to the fashion industry, "fast fashion" and its endless production of clothes is being called into question. This is largely due to the huge amount of resources needed and waste generated. Even energy consumption is evolving: energy cooperatives have appeared in Northern Europe where consumers take on the role of prosumers who strictly monitor their energy production and consumption.

These changes have undeniably been fostered by the younger generations. As previously mentioned, Millennials have shaken up mainstream consumption habits by engaging in alternative and disruptive consumer practices with peer-to-peer sharing platforms, collaborative models of all sorts, including second-hand purchasing, product to service schemes, veganism, etc. Instead of acquiring a product to fulfil a specific need, these new consumers prefer to access a service and become a member of a sharing community. In this respect, the relative decline of mass retail in Europe and North America is a case in point.

At this point, critical voices will obviously appear and easily discard the above demonstration. How can you talk about major changes in consumer habits when millions of new middle class citizens from the developing world are frantically buying Western brands and acquiring Western status symbols with little regard for the social and environmental dimensions? Or when millions of Bottom of Pyramid consumers are desperately seeking to get out of poverty?

As the sustainability movement shows, developing countries may not follow the same path as their counterparts in developed countries did in the space of just over a century. In other words, it is far from certain that educated consumers in the developing world will remain fascinated by Western lifestyles for long! With the constant circulation of information around the world, the harmonization of educational patterns and the side effects of globalization, one can predict that consumers in developing countries will soon see the downsides of a Western lifestyle. Moreover, Millennials and the Z Generation all over the world share the same concerns.

In addition, consumers in the developing world are increasingly concerned with environmental and social scandals: from contaminated milk in China to pesticide use in India and Latin America, sustainability-related awareness is gaining momentum everywhere. Moreover, a growing number of people are gradually reverting to more traditional, local consumption habits. Western brands especially for food and clothing are no longer necessarily the most attractive ... And this may also be true in other areas such as housing, energy and manufacturing, to name but a few.

Faced with changing consumption patterns, multinationals especially must cope with complex challenges. In their quest to reinvent themselves, propose brand new products and services, and rethink their business models and supply chains, businesses are relying on profound medium-term changes in consumption patterns. Sustainability-driven CSR is clearly one of the key responses to new consumer expectations, but this may push companies into unchartered waters, which could possibly jeopardize their financial sustainability...

Unilever and Pepsico are prime examples. Former Unilever CEO Paul Polman insisted on the need for multinationals to engage in multi-stakeholder coalitions in an effort to provide long-term solutions for a sustainable world.[12] Yet, one may wonder if the brand portfolio of the company is not in itself an obstacle to this aim given its diversity and complexity. Secondly, it is difficult not to be skeptical towards former Pepsico CEO Indra Nooyi's statement that she wants her company to be a model sustainable company when one sees the type of brands the multinational sells.

This leads us to question the inherent logic of sustainability-driven CSR: indeed, how can one draw the line between companies which may become sustainable and those which may not? Can making cement or steel be sustainable? What does sustainability mean for oil and gas companies? Is it possible for companies selling fast fashion and unhealthy products to become truly sustainable?

One may even wonder if the same reasoning applies if we examine CSR in its more traditional form: we may ask if a tobacco company can be considered socially responsible? Ultimately, deploying CSR always further in our present world leads to fundamentally question our very needs, i.e. the society in which we wish to live. This is likely to be one of the main challenges in the years to come: if questioning our needs leads us to question the business world as it is today, we may wonder to what extent big globalized companies will still be legitimate... We may well see the return of smaller local community-based businesses as favored forms of production and service-providers, in which case, CSR would appear to be a concept from the past...

---

[12] Paul Polman, A Business Model for Sustainability, *Project Syndicate*, December 2018, available at https://www.project-syndicate.org/commentary/business-model-for-sustainable-development-by-paul-polman-2018–12?barrier=accesspaylog.

CONCLUSION

In conclusion let us first look at some key learnings about CSR and its current evolution.

CSR past, present and future

CSR is a constantly evolving concept which remains nebulous due to its historical and geographical development, as well as to the diversity of the issues it encompasses today. One can clearly distinguish between the historic form of CSR, born in the U.S. in the 1950s and based on the national philanthropic-ethical tradition, and the European-sponsored sustainability-driven form which emerged in the wake of the sustainable development concept in the early 1990s. Both these forms are currently hybridizing in the wake of the globalization process and the constitution of global value chains.

As a result, CSR serves very diverse needs today, from giving back to society through financial donations to the strategic embeddedness of some key CSR issues usually related to environmentally sustainable product developments. Most businesses today are neither focused solely on giving back nor on embedding sustainability: a large majority of them are engaged in a form of compliance-driven CSR characterized by mimetic approaches and the inclusion of international soft law standards and instruments. In this respect, it shall be interesting to see whether the 17 Sustainable Development Goals live up to their promise of genuinely engaging the private and public sectors in cooperating to find solutions to the sustainability challenge.

Especially critical will be the evolution of CSR in the developing world: although one can bet on some hybrid forms taking shape, we genuinely believe that socially-driven sustainability could be a key driver to embed CSR in corporate strategies and operations. This, of course, does not mean that environmentally-driven sustainability ought to be neglected, yet social issues are urgent matters that must be tackled efficiently by businesses, be they the subsidiaries of multinationals or locally-rooted businesses.

As for the evolution of CSR in the coming decade, our assumption is that two main distinct forms will emerge: the *social responsibility approach*, focused on philanthropy but in an updated way, i.e. more strategic and associated with a series of compliance-based policies, and *corporate sustainability strategies* aimed at a profound transformation of business models. While the first type may respond to some short to medium term needs and expectations, our belief is that only corporate sustainability will be able to find long-term efficient responses to the sustainability challenge.

However, this will only be made possible if companies are capable of innovating in a disruptive way, which implies collaborating with civil society organizations, social enterprises and start-ups as well as public actors. In this matter, multinationals must exert their responsibility since they have the means to invest in new disruptive social and environmental innovations. In doing so, they will gain new competences and new mindsets.

Eventually the concept of CSR as it is today is likely to fade and give way to two distinct types of responsible corporate behavior, one being essentially founded on the willingness to donate and help society, the other recognizing that the business world needs to transform to become a key provider of sustainability-related solutions. All these assumptions depend largely on consumption patterns and demands. In truth, business transformation toward sustainability is really conditioned upon profound changes in our lifestyles around the world!

How to walk the talk on stakeholders

It is taken for granted now that CSR is inherently linked to a stakeholder approach. How can a company determine what its key issues are without reviewing the demands and expectations of its key stakeholders? As we have seen, stakeholder analysis has become quite commonplace today, even in developing countries. Yet, there is still a long way to go to move from stakeholder review to stakeholder inclusion and management. Fully taking into account stakeholders does not seem feasible as long as corporate practice continues to adhere to the dominant shareholder-based governance models. However, there are many positive signs today from a legal and governance-related perspective that should push the stakeholder further up the agenda.

In this respect, we thought it was important to stress the urgent need to take employees and their representatives into account more when engaging in CSR policies. Whereas they play a crucial role especially in developing countries, trade unions are definitely a blind spot of CSR today. Even when it comes to employee involvement, generally speaking, CSR theory and practice do not provide much insight. An especially critical dimension of CSR is the cultural context which has been long neglected or at least underestimated. Indeed, norms and societal constructs play a crucial role in the diffusion of CSR.

Two strategic priorities on today's agenda

After going through the CSR agenda as a whole, it appears that two topics are of prime importance for companies that would like to make a difference in their CSR approach. The first one is the human rights question which has been attracting a lot of attention over the last few years. This is a crucial point given the impact of human rights issues around the world due to globalization and intricate supply chains. Even though very few multinationals have truly grasped the strategic importance of human rights, the question is bound to become a major challenge for multinationals. Moreover, it has become clear since the Ruggie principles established a decade ago that multinationals and national governments must take responsibility in the fight against human rights violations and abuses.

The second priority issue is related to the urgent need for companies to learn from nature so as to move beyond compliance and embed environmental sustainability in their core strategy up until their business models are radically transformed. Circular approaches, biomimicry, and sustainable innovations are gradually leading to a paradigm shift: our classical linear production-consumption pattern is being challenged at last, and we are moving toward an economic model based on ecological patterns.

In the end, what is at stake is the core definition of sustainability and responsibility. We must determine the contours of sustainable and responsible businesses. Indeed, sustainability and responsibility are intrinsically connected, and both terms exemplify the key challenges for the business world so often criticized for its lack of ethical and socially responsible conduct. Let us now try to define what the ideal sustainable and responsible business would look like.

Imagining the ideal sustainable and responsible business

Becoming sustainable for any company today is a formidable challenge: indeed, a truly sustainable business constantly aims to optimize its performance regarding profits, the planet and people. It is therefore essential to succeed in enhancing positive social and environmental impacts, while also maintaining economic efficiency and financial profitability. Ultimately, companies are bound to rethink their whole business model while taking into consideration all the potential consequences, such as the need to radically transform their products and services. To do this, a long-term vision is a prerequisite. This is also true for top management: without a personally committed CEO, the sustainability challenge will remain on a distant horizon. A sustainability-driven strategy might even lead a company to reconsider the legal and governance structure so as to get the full support of shareholders.

As for being a responsible company, the stakes are also high. Indeed, responsibility extends far beyond the habitual legal and even ethical boundaries. "Responsible business" refers to the company's ability to make the right decisions today while taking into account the future. This new ethics of responsibility requires companies to have a clear vision of social and environmental challenges ahead in order to be able to resist short-term market pressures and bet on a long-term "return". Only by adopting this "backcasting" approach will companies be able to take part in overcoming urgent challenges such as climate change or loss of biodiversity. Being responsible also refers to the entire value chain.

Multinationals especially are required to endorse full responsibility for what may happen at the very end of their outsourced supply chain.

Such an ideal company is hard to find. More broadly speaking, a genuine shift in paradigm and mindset is needed. Truly grasping the profound evolutions of society, listening to stakeholders and partnering with outsiders are major challenges for most businesses today. Being fully accountable for all of the actions and policies undertaken to be a socially responsible company requires humility, consistency and a constant pursuit of improvement and positive contributions for the common good. Let us hope that more and more companies all around the world will follow suit and set the course for the future! Our world needs them...

SELECTED BIBLIOGRAPHY

Acosta Collazos, M., Acquier, A. & Delbard, O.: "Just Do It? The Adoption of Sustainable Supply Chain Management Programs from a Supplier Perspective", *Supply Chain Forum: An International Journal*, 15(1), pp. 76–91, 2014.

Acquier, A., Gond, J.P. & Pasquero, J.: "Rediscovering Howard Bowen's Social Responsibilities of the Businessman", *Business & Society*, 2011.

Aguilera & Jackson: "The Cross-National Diversity of Corporate Governance: Dimensions and Determinants", *Academy of Management Review*, 28(3), pp. 447–465, 2003.

Anderson, R.: *Confessions of a Radical Industrialist*, rh, Business Books, 2009.

Austin, J.: "Strategic Collaboration Between Nonprofits and Business", *Nonprofit and Voluntary Sector Quaterly*, 29(1), pp. 69–97, 2001.

Benyus, J.: *Biomimicry: Innovation Inspired by Nature*, Harper Perrenial, 2002.

Bowen, Howard R.: *Social Responsibilities of the Businessman*, University of Iowa Press, Iowa city, first edition 1953, new edition 2013.

Boulding, K.E.: "The Economics of the Coming Spaceship Earth." *Environmental Quality Issues in a Growing Economy*, In H. Jarrett (ed.), 1966.

Capron, M.: "History, Challenges and Limitations of the 'Corporate Social Responsibility' and 'Sustainable Development' Coupling" (with F. Quairel-Lanoizelée), *in* J.M. Lasry, Lautier D., Fessler D. (eds.), *The Economics of Sustainable Development*, Economica, pp. 341–359, 2010.

Carnegie, A.: *The Gospel of Wealth and Other Writings*, New York, Penguin Books, first published in 1889.

Carroll, A.B.: "A Three Dimensional Model of Corporate Social Performance", *Academy of Management Review*, pp. 497–505, 1979.

Carroll, A.B.: "Corporate Social Responsibility — Evolution of a definitional construct", *Business and Society*, pp. 268–295, 1999.

Chouinard, Y.: *Let My People Go Surfing: The Education of a Reluctant Businessman*, Penguin Books, 2006.

Clarkson, M.B.: "A Stakeholder Framework for Analyzing and Evaluating Corporate Social Performance", *The Academy of Management Review*, 20(1), pp. 92–117, 1995.

Costanza, R.: "Ecological Economics: Reintegrating the Study of Humans and Nature", *Ecological Applications*, 6(4), pp. 978–990, 1996.

Crane, A., Mcwilliams, A., Matten, D., Moon, J. & Siegel, D.S.: *The Oxford Handbook of Corporate Social Responsibility*. New York, NY: Oxford University Press, 2009.

Crane, A., Palazzo, B. & Matten, D.: "Contesting the Value of "Creating Shared Value"", *California Management Review*, 56, 2014.

Dahlsrud, A.: "How Corporate Social Responsibility is Defined: An Analysis of 37 Definitions", *Corporate Social Responsibility and Environmental Management*, 2006.

Daly, H.: *Steady-State Economics* (2nd ed.), Island Press, 1977, 1991.

Delbard, O.: "Social Partners of Full-Fledged Stakeholders? Trade Unions and CSR in Europe", *Society and Business Review*, 6, pp. 260–277, 2011.

Dillard, J. et al.: *Corporate Social Responsibility: A Research Handbook*, Routledge, 2014.

DiMaggio, P.J. & Powell, W.W.: "The Iron Cage Revisited: Institutional Isomorphism and Collective Rationality in Organisational Fields", *American Sociological Review*, pp. 147–160, 1983.

Djelic, M.L.: *Exporting the American Model: The Post-war Transformation of European Businesses*, Oxford, Oxford University Press, 1998.

Donaldson, T. & Preston, L.E.: "The Stakeholder Theory of the Corporation: Concepts, Evidence, and Implications", *The Academy of Management Review*, 20(1), pp. 65–91, 1995.

Elkington, J.: *Cannibals with Forks: The Triple Bottom Line of 21st Century Business*, Capstone/John Wiley, 1997.

Emerson, J.: *"Maximizing Blended Value — Building Beyond the Blended Value Map to Sustainable Investing, Philanthropy, and Organization"*, blendedvalue.org, 2005.

Freeman, R.E.: *Strategic Management — A Stakeholder Approach*, Pitman Publishing, 1984.

Frederick, W.: From CSR1 to CSR2 — "The Maturing of Business-and-Society Thought", University of Pitsburgh, *Working Paper 279*, 1978.

Friedman, M.: "The social responsibility of business is to increase its profits", *New York Times Magazine*, September 13, 1970.

Garriga, E. & Melé, D.: "Corporate Social Responsibility Theories: Mapping the Territory", *Journal of Business Ethics*, pp. 51–71, 2004.

Georgescu-Roegen, N.: *The Entropy Law and the Economic Process,* Harvard University Press, 1971.

Gond, J.P. & Matten, D.: "Rethinking the Business-Society Interface — Beyond the Functionalist Trap", No. 47–2007 *ICCSR Research Paper Series,* International Centre for Corporate Social Responsibility, Nottingham University Business School, Nottingham University, 2007.

Habisch, A. *et al.*: *CSR Across Europe,* Berlin, Springer, 2004.

Hawken, P.: *The Ecology of Commerce: A Declaration of Sustainability,* Harper Business, 1993, 2010 (revised edition).

Hawken, P., Lovins, H, Lovins, A*: Natural Capitalism: Creating the Next Industrial Revolution,* U.S. Green Building Council, 2000.

Hawken, P.: *Project Drawdown,* Penguin Books, 2017.

Heald, M.: "Management's Responsibility to Society: The Growth of an Idea", *The Business History Review,* 31(4) (Winter, 1957), pp. 375–384.

Hollingsworth, J.R. & Boyer, R.: *Contemporary Capitalism: The Embeddedness of Institutions,* Cambridge, Cambridge University Press, 1997.

Holzer, B.: "Turning Stakeseekers Into Stakeholders", *Business and Society,* 47(1), pp. 50–67, 2008.

Husted, B.W. & Allen, D.B.: "Corporate social responsibility in the multinational enterprise: strategic and institutional approaches", *Journal of International Business Studies,* 37(6), pp. 838–849, 2006.

Jamali, D. & Keshishian, T.: "Uneasy Alliances: Lessons Learned from Partnerships Between Businesses and NGOs in the Context of CSR", *Journal of Business Ethics,* 84(2), pp. 277–295, 2009.

Kahn, F. & Lund-Thomsen, P.: "CSR as Imperialism: Towards a Phenomenological Approach to CSR In the Developing World", *Journal of Change Management,* 11(1), pp. 73–90, 2011.

Levitt, T.: "The Dangers of Social Responsibility", *Harvard Business Review,* 1958.

Löfstedt, R.E. & Vogel, D.: "The Changing Character of Regulation: A Comparison of Europe and the United States", *Risk Analysis,* pp. 399–405, 2001.

Lovins, A. & Braungart, M.: "A New Dynamic — Effective Business in a Circular Economy", *Ellen MacArthur Foundation Publishing,* 2014.

March, J. & Olsen, J.: *Rediscovering Institutions: The Organisational Basis of Politics,* New York, Free Press, 1989.

Margolis, J. & Walsh, J.: "Misery Loves Companies: Rethinking Social Initiatives by Business", *Administrative Science Quarterly,* 48(2), pp. 268–305, 2003.

Matten, D. & Crane, A.: "Corporate Citizenship: Toward an Extented Theoretical Conceptualization", *Academy of Management Review,* pp. 166–179, 2005.

Matten, D. & Moon, J.: "'Implicit' and 'Explicit' CSR: A Conceptual Framework for a Comparative Understanding of Corporate Social Responsibility", *The Academy of Management Review*, pp. 404–424, 2008.

Matten, D. & Moon, J.: "Corporate Social Responsibility Education in Europe", *Journal of Business Ethics*, pp. 232–337, 2004.

Mcdonough, W. & Braungart, M.: *Cradle to Cradle: Remaking the Way We Make Things*. MacMillan, 2010.

Meadows, D, Meadows, D *et al.*: *The Limits to Growth*, Universe Books, 1972.

Mitchell, R., Agle, B. & Wood, D.: "Toward a Theory of Stakeholder Identification and Salience: Defining the Principle of Who and What Really Counts", *The Academy of Management Review*, 22(4), pp. 853–886, 1997.

Moon, J., Crane, A. & Matten, D.: "Can Corporations Be Citizens? Corporate Citizenship as a Metaphor for Business Participation in Society", *Business Ethics Quaterly*, pp. 427–451, 2005.

Nidumolu, R., Prahalad, C.K., & Rangaswami, M.R.: "Why Sustainability is Now the Key Driver of Innovation", *Harvard Business Review*, 87(9), pp. 56–64, 2009.

Orsato, R.: "Competitive Environmental Strategies: When Does It Pay to Be Green?", *California Management Review*, 48(2), 2006.

Pauli, G.: "The Blue Economy"', *Our Planet*, pp. 24–27, 2010.

Porter, M. & Kramer, M.: "Strategy and Society: The Link Between Competitive Advantage and Corporate Social Responsibility", *Harvard Business Review*, pp. 78–92, 2006.

Porter, M. & Kramer, M.: "The Competitive Advantage of Corporate Philanthropy", *Harvard Business Review*, Winter 2002.

Porter, M. & Kramer, M.: "Creating Shared Value", *Harvard Business Review*, 89(1/2), pp. 62–77, 2011.

Prahalad, C.K.: *The Fortune at the Bottom of the Pyramid*, Upper Saddle River, Wharton School of Publishing, 2005.

Preuss, L., Haunschild, A. & Matten, D.: "Trade Unions and CSR: A European Research Agenda", *Journal of Public Affairs*, 6(3–4), 2006.

Preuss, L.: "A Reluctant Stakeholder? On the Perception of Corporate Social Responsibility Among European Trade Unions", *Business Ethics: A European Review*, 17, 2008.

Roddick, A.: *Business as Unusual*, Thorsons, 2001.

Rosanvallon, P.: Democratic Universalism as a Historical Problem", doi.org, 2009.

Scherer, A. & Palazzo, G.: "Toward a Political Conception of Corporate Responsibility: Business and Society Seen from a Habermasian Perspective", *The Academy of Management Review*, 32(4), pp. 1096–1120, 2007.

Selski, J. & Parker, P.: "Cross-Sector Partnerships to Address Social Issues: Challenges to Theory and Practice", *Journal of Management*, 31(6), pp. 849–873, 2005.

Tempel, A. & Walgenbach, P.: "Global Standardization of Organizational Forms and Management Practices? What New Institutionalism and the Business-Systems Approach Can Learn from Each Other", *Journal of Management Studies*, pp. 1–24, 2007.

Vogel, D.: "The Globalization of Business Ethics: Why America Remains Different", *California Management Review*, pp. 30–49, 1992.

Willard, B.: *The New Sustainability Advantage: Seven Business Case Benefits of a Triple Bottom Line*, New Society Publishers, 2012.

Whitley R. (Ed.): *European Business Systems*, London, Sage, 1997.

Wood D.J.: "Corporate Social Performance Revisited", *The Academy of Management Review*, 16(4), 1991.

Zadek S.: *The Civil Corporation*, Routledge, 2007.

INDEX

169